The Posters That Won The War

Derek Nelson

Motorbooks International
Publishers & Wholesalers ®

First published in 1991 by Motorbooks International
Publishers & Wholesalers, P O Box 2, 729 Prospect Avenue,
Osceola, WI 54020 USA

The information in this book is true and complete to the
best of our knowledge. All recommendations are made
without any guarantee on the part of the author or
publisher, who also disclaim any liability incurred in
connection with the use of this data or specific details

We recognize that some words, model names and
designations, for example, mentioned herein are the
property of the trademark holder. We use them for
identification purposes only. This is not an official
publication

Motorbooks International books are also available at
discounts in bulk quantity for industrial or sales-
promotional use. For details write to Special Sales Manager
at the Publisher's address

Library of Congress Cataloging-in-Publication Data
Nelson, Derek.
    The posters that won the war / Derek Nelson.
       p.   cm.
    ISBN 0-87938-515-4
    1. World War, 1939–1945—Posters.   2. World War,
1939–1945—Propaganda.   3. Propaganda, American—
History—20th century.
I. Title.
D743.25.N45 1991
940.54′88673—dc20   90-23798

On the front cover: A War Bond poster by an artist named
Wilkinson.

Printed and bound in Hong Kong

Contents

Acknowledgments

My deepest appreciation to the staff at the War Memorial Museum of Virginia in Newport News, Virginia. Thanks to director John Quarstein, for his enthusiasm about the project, and especially to registrar Bill Barker, for his indefatigable assistance with research and photography. Barker cheerfully applied his unusual expertise to identify the significance of posters and to educate me about military lore in general.

The War Memorial Museum of Virginia is operated by the city of Newport News and maintains an excellent permanent exhibit of posters. Unless otherwise noted, the posters and photos in this book are from that museum and reflect only a small part of its outstanding collection.

Sincere thanks to the following people, who helped untangle some of the thickets of archives along the way: David Pfeiffer, Washington National Records Center, Suitland, Maryland; Maja Felaco, reference specialist, Prints and Photographs Division, Library of Congress, Washington, DC; Mary Beth Straight, assistant photo archivist, and Linda Cullen, librarian, United States Naval Institute, Annapolis, Maryland; and Mark Weber, Naval Historical Center, Washington, DC.

Thanks also to my editor at Motorbooks, Greg Field, for his vision and enthusiasm about this project, and to copy editor Cheryl Drivdahl, who gave the text clarity and consistency.

As always, my final thanks to my wife, Mary, and my son, Nate, for their patience and for giving me time and space to pursue this work.

This book is dedicated to the Acme Pie Company, one of the thousands of places that displayed posters during World War II.

Introduction

Family Photos for "the Smartest, Toughest, Luckiest, Leanest, All-Around Knowingest Nation on God's Green Earth"

For something so ostensibly simple—an image, a slogan, a splash of color—the poster has generated a surprising amount of controversy. For something intended to be so clear, it can be quite deceptive.

Posters have more to them than meets the eye. They offer an invaluable historical text, since they reflect the shifting hopes and fears of countries at war. They offer a virtual catalog of propaganda techniques, aimed at bolstering friends and discouraging enemies. They also offer clear insight into a country's sociology, its cultural roots, its folklore and its prejudices. And apart from these intellectual concerns, posters can be appreciated simply as well-designed—or amateurish—visual entities.

The central debate between defenders and detractors of posters is whether posters are art or advertisement. If both, where does one role start and the other end? Can posters only "sell," or can they teach and inspire? The critics, the connoisseurs, the people who collect posters and the people who create them all seem to disagree.

However, no one disputes one thing: Posters are popular. Posters and billboards are widely accepted as offering the quickest and most reliable insights into a country's events and preoccupations. They have been a visible and familiar part of the United States' visual landscape for a century. Posters were particularly prominent during World War II, when the military services, civilian groups and all levels of government called upon them to serve dozens of needs and to play an astonishing variety of roles. Posters announced, exhorted, scolded and amused. They instructed, guided and ordered. They produced, in viewers, feelings of power, sorrow, guilt and fury.

Although the topics and techniques of the posters changed during the course of the war, the posters themselves are only tenuously linked to the military progress of the conflict. The posters were aimed at the folks back home and only rarely at the soldiers in camps or foxholes. Thus, although soldiers are a dominant image in

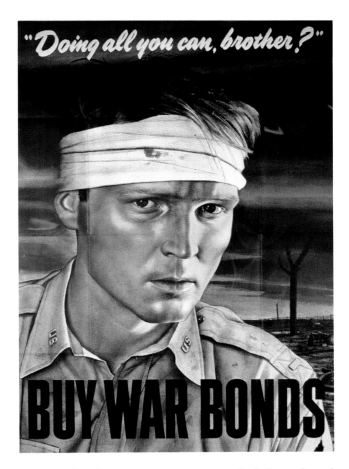

Compared with most recruiting posters, which showed good-looking, muscular soldiers, this vision of a wounded soldier had strong impact. One major genre of posters aimed to cheer up and encourage the folks at home. This poster belongs in an alternative genre, with its thinly veiled accusation that some civilians were slacking or coasting. Robert Sloan made this poster in 1943. Sloan did a number of posters for the Treasury Department, as well as covers and portraits for Time *and* Coronet *magazines.*

them, they aim to communicate to mothers and grand-parents, industrial workers and civilians at large.

The intended audience of the posters, as well as the let's-get-'em, gung ho mood of the times, is neatly expressed by Lauren Lyman, assistant to the president of United Aircraft Corporation, in this passage from the 1942 book *America Organizes to Win the War:* "Men and women, many of them novices, are working with all their strength to provide the air power that is striking power. Folks from the farms; girls from offices; boys from school and college, from city streets and mountain villages; youngsters just out of school; old men who thought they had retired—they are all there together, all playing the greatest game of their lives on the varsity team of Democracy, playing with no time out, as con-

Although the term GI later came to refer to a soldier, at this point in the war it still meant "government issue," here refer- ring to the soldier's gear. This is a rare poster aimed at the troops, as opposed to the folks back home. Albert Dorne did it for the Army Conservation Program in 1943. The sergeant in the picture wears a pair of yellow campaign badges over his right pocket. Note the poster within a poster, an unusual approach.

secrated to victory, and as necessary to it, as the pilots who will actually fly the planes they, the workers, are making."

The messages aimed at this audience were impor- tant. According to historian D'Ann Campbell in *Women at War with America,* "Passive resistance to the war in the form of tax evasion, refusal to buy bonds, or participation in the black market could have seriously weakened the war effort, and concern over this possi- bility led to far tighter governmental controls on the lives of the people. The Office of War Information (OWI) constantly monitored the mood of consumers," issuing hundreds of posters in response to its findings. Campbell wrote, "Keeping up the pitch of activity on the home front was a constant challenge, which proba- bly increased in difficulty as the war progressed and victory became simply a matter of time." This chal- lenge explains the tremendous redundancy of posters, and the continued reappearance of similar topics throughout the four years of the war. Even when the war ended, for example, plenty of bills needed to be paid.

On the one hand was the government, which had specific tasks it needed specific parts of the civilian population to do. On the other hand were millions of citizens who wanted to get involved in the war effort. The match between the two wasn't always perfect. The result was a great many nebulous posters whose goal was to boost morale. "Many strategists saw the civilian population as the weakest element in national defense. Lacking military training, leadership, and discipline, the civilian would be less prepared to cope, his morale could be more easily shattered," historian Lee Kennett wrote in *For the Duration* (1985). Numerous posters were aimed simply at bucking the civilian up. The "loose lips sink ships" genre of poster let people feel involved in the war effort while doing nothing at all.

Even though the posters are sometimes blunt and graphic, on the whole they are not snapshots of reality. More often, they reflect what the government hoped would *become* reality. Art historian John Barnicoat in *A Concise History of Posters,* underlines this in his discus- sion of posters as an expression of the "popular idiom," which had, he wrote, "two main directional currents. One flows upwards from the level of folk art and brings with it a common factor of integrity and a certain naivety. The other current flows downward and is usu- ally called mass culture; it is commercial or political propaganda, pre-digested and made palatable for mass-consumption." Posters produced by the govern- ment, he pointed out, are "made to seem a true reflec- tion of the popular condition," when in fact they are "a projection from the forces in power." When a poster

Next page
Here is another of the small subset of posters aimed at sol- diers. Depending on how tired you were, the gas mask actu- ally made a decent pillow.

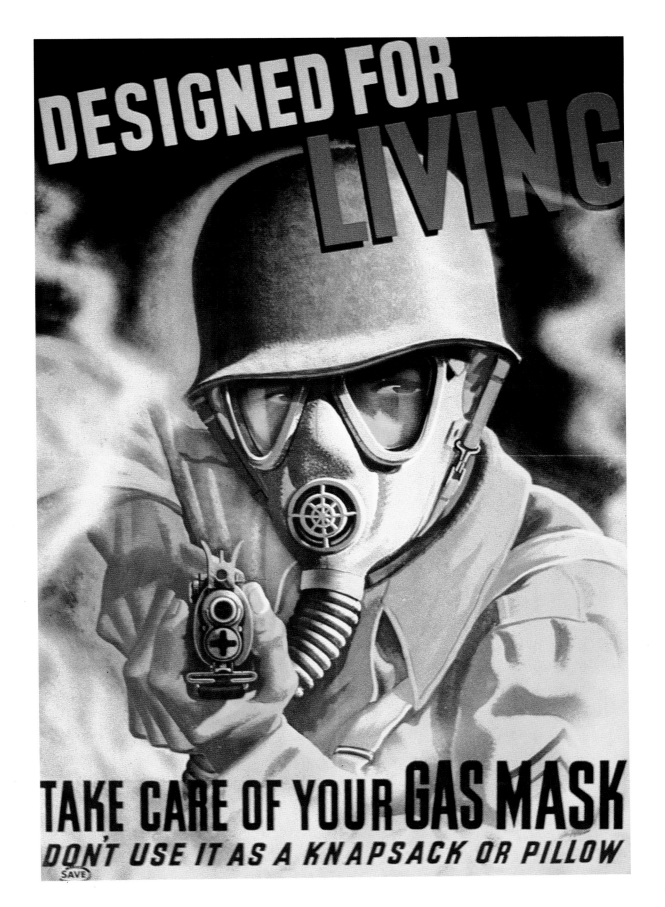

Although everyone knew that soldiers were killed and wounded in battle, official representations of those facts were rare early in the war. This poster, from the War Production Board, sounds the familiar theme of worker as soldier. Labor management committees were extremely active and useful in keeping organized labor cheerfully committed to the tasks at hand when the usual labor management rules were suspended. Issued in 1943, this is WPB poster number A–35.

shows a war hero who is black, for example, it certainly doesn't mean that ethnic prejudice wasn't a problem. In fact, ethnic prejudice was a severe problem, and the poster was issued in an effort to combat it.

The roles that women played during the war eventually find diverse expression in the posters. The accuracy of that expression is open to discussion. According to some critics, the frequency and the perspective of the images shown in the posters distort the reality. "The media, closely following directives from Washington, glorified martial values, and saluted women chiefly when they took on traditionally male roles as soldiers, fliers or riveters," D'Ann Campbell wrote. "Yet studying the image of the American Woman, whether that projected by the movies, soap operas, novels, billboards, women's magazines, daily press, or government propaganda, only offers a very indirect access to American women's actual experiences." Nevertheless, we see Women Accepted for Volunteer Emergency Service (WAVES), nurses, workers, mothers, shoppers

in the posters. The variety of these roles far surpasses that of men's roles.

When analyzing a poster's message, you have to look at the motive behind the surface statement. Some people didn't do what the posters told them to do. In the case of victory gardens, the government couldn't lick 'em so it joined 'em. Before the war, the Department of Agriculture tried strongly to dissuade city dwellers and other nonrural folks from planting gardens. American farmers were producing plenty of food and much more efficiently than home gardeners could. Nevertheless, millions of people started plowing up their yard. Soon, victory gardens appeared on posters as officially approved wartime projects.

Posters are rarely subtle. They are executed with a broad brush, in terms of both media and message. They tend to be bright, loud, startling, even shocking. To some extent, this approach meshes perfectly with the philosophical tendencies of the war itself. Someone was either friend or foe. The Allies were right, the Axis was wrong. There were no shades in between.

You grasp this flavor in the foreword to the book *America Organizes to Win the War*. Here's how the publishers described the years before the outbreak of war in Europe: "The aggressors had spent most of a tragic decade destroying democracy in Europe and Asia and waging brutal wars of conquest against weaker peoples on three continents. . . . [B]ecause the world had not been made safe for democracy, the people of the United States were summoned to new sacrifices of blood and treasure on a scale vastly greater

This powerful image would have shocked viewers early in the war, when the folks at home were sheltered from images of wounded or dead soldiers. Here presented as a poster, it also *appeared in public-service advertisements later in the war.* National Archives

Previous page
This poster offers a good example of the sort of domestic symbolism that would be immediately familiar to Americans but would probably mystify people from other countries. The use of historical figures was a common technique in war posters, particularly during World War I. This is OWI poster number 26, issued in 1943. The poster was created by Bernard Perlin and David Stone Martin.

than that of 1917." In a speech on December 9, 1941, President Franklin D. Roosevelt disposed of the Axis as "powerful and resourceful gangsters [who] have banded together to make war upon the whole human race."

These gangsters are the verbal counterparts of the grotesque caricatures of Japanese and Germans that inhabit some posters. Posters tend to deal in archetypes and stereotypes, exaggerated images and icons. Those things are the poster's normal vocabulary; as you study enough posters, you get used to their garish idiom and come to expect it. As Zbynek Zeman pointed out in *Selling the War* (1978), "Every nation portrays its warriors as noble, its women as compassionate and virtuous, its war aims as righteous. The enemy, on the other hand, is portrayed as misguided, evil, fighting for an ignoble cause."

Posters tend to simplify matters. They don't give us essays or closely reasoned debates, they give us slogans. They do so to such an extent that Lee Kennett wrote, "The history of the first six months of the war could be written in slogans, beginning with 'Remember Pearl Harbor'—coined in the first hours of the war, and apparently in a score of places at once"—and continuing on through "Tin to Win," "Vitamins for Victory" and dozens of others.

This tendency to simplify things is a two-edged sword and helps explain both the strengths and weaknesses of posters. Posters can cut right to the heart of a matter, but they can also miss the mark entirely: they become overly idealistic, ultracorny, obscure, overbearing, even bizarre. Especially early in the war, many government pronouncements, including posters, were criticized as at best unrealistic and at worst simply deceptive. According to Kennett, "By 1944, pollster William Lydgate maintained apathy, or at least a sense of detachment from the war, was a very real problem, which he laid at the door of the administration. It coddled and babied the public with an oversanitized version of the war, so that many could not see the need for sacrifice." Exceptions certainly exist, but Lydgate's findings may help explain why posters had to keep trying so hard, and why the huge federal poster dynamo worked overtime throughout the war.

Posters for war bonds, recruiting and industrial production dominate any selection. Some posters take less tangible ideas as their subject. They deal, sometimes symbolically, with such things as democracy and religion, in a way that may sound peculiar to modern ears. Archibald MacLeish wrote in *The American*

Cause in 1941, "To mobilize planes only or armies only, forgetting our purposes as a democratic people, interrupting our history, neglecting the realization of our own hopes, is to invite disaster." These stirring pronouncements were an intrinsic part of the experience of the war, which was once again aimed at making the world safe for democracy.

To understand the enthusiasms of the war years, you must realize that the word *democracy* meant more than a type of political system. Speaking of Americans in the 1830s and 1840s, MacLeish wrote, "They knew what democracy was. They knew what they were too. They were the smartest, toughest, luckiest, leanest, all-around knowingest nation on God's green earth. Their way of living was the handsomest way of living human beings had ever hit on. Their institutions were the institutions history had been waiting for." Beliefs such as this one carried Americans through the early, dark months of the conflict and through the hard, painful years after.

Author Geoffrey Perrett called *Days of Sadness, Years of Triumph*, his novel about the war, "the story of how a nation that stumbled into 1939 shaken, divided, confused and unhappy was in a sense remade, so that only six years later it was strong, united, happy and confident as never before or since." Posters were a tool that figured into that remaking. In the summer of 1942, the OWI's Special Services Division studied the war's effects on the family. Among the many pros and cons were two interesting, perhaps predictable findings: the war seemed to give purpose to people, and it increased the sense of community.

"To Americans the test of almost anything is how well it works, not whether it is old, or divine, or popular," Perrett wrote. "The war years provided the last great collective social experience in the country's history, and when at the end of the war the United States bestrode the entire world like a colossus, it had proved itself to its own people."

The posters in this book are the family photos of that colossus.

Next page
Almost fifty years later, it is difficult to fully appreciate America's outrage at the attack on Pearl Harbor. On December 7, 1941, the Japanese ambassador gave a document to the US secretary of state that was ostensibly a reply to a US proposal for peace in the Pacific, which had been delivered on November 26. The Japanese reply came an hour after the attack on Pearl Harbor. The secretary of state described the document thusly:

> *In my fifty years of public service I have never seen a document that was more crowded with infamous falsehoods and distortions—infamous falsehoods and distortions on a scale so huge that I never imagined until today that any Government on this planet was capable of uttering them*

This poster was issued in 1942. The quote on the poster is from the end of Lincoln's Gettysburg Address. The artist was Allen Saalburg.

...we here highly resolve that these dead shall not have died in vain...

REMEMBER DEC. 7th!

Strong in the strength of the Lord we who fight in the people's cause will never stop until that cause is won

This 1942 poster by David Stone Martin was issued as OWI poster number 8. The quote is from a speech by Vice President Henry Wallace. Religious symbols are rare in posters of World War II, although most combatants assume the God-is-on-our-side role sooner or later. Nevertheless, the campaign against the Axis clearly had spiritual, as opposed to simply political, overtones to many Americans. In The American Cause (1941), Archibald MacLeish, a poet and head of the Office of Facts and Figures, wrote, "The issue which divides our time is far more than the issue between armed forces. History has shown us that it is an issue between worlds: an issue which depends more surely on our souls than on our weapons. . . . We are wondering whether democracy in the United States has other spiritual weapons than the doubts and misgivings which ten years of depression and twenty years of skepticism provided for the men of France to fight with."

In July 1940, Pearl Harbor was still far in the future and public opinion vacillated over whether the United States would have to intervene or not. This pedestrian seemed to be saying, "Who, me?" when he confronted James Montgomery Flagg's famous poster in Benton Harbor, Michigan. This poster was in front of a post office. In the distance at the right is a well-known poster by Howard Chandler Christy. Both the Flagg and Christy posters were originally issued during World War I, the latter in 1918. Flagg's poster was inspired by a World War I British poster by Alfred Leete, which showed Lord Kitchener in a similar, stern pose. Originally, Flagg created his design for the cover of Leslie's Weekly. More than 4 million copies of Flagg's version were printed during World War I, and some sources say that 5 million were produced during World War II, when the poster was used by the Army Recruiting Publicity Bureau starting in 1940. Flagg was both prolific and durable—his career spanned fifty years, and he produced more than 300 illustrations per year during his prime. John Vachon made this photo for the Office of War Information. Library of Congress.

Chapter 1

The Folks Back Home

"Confident of Victory, Dazzled by Cataclysm"

Since posters reflect specific trends and forces in contemporary society, current events provide the context for understanding and appreciating them. During World War II, the fabric of American life was transformed in a manner that was unequaled before and has been unequaled since. Consumers had to drastically change their habits, although some older citizens merely had to dust off the home-front customs of World War I. Just when it seemed as if the Depression was put behind us, grim reminders cropped up during every trip to the grocery store and with every government news release. Government influence and control mushroomed. Plenty of jobs were available—sometimes too many—but not always in the localities where workers were. And always there was a sense of urgency—to do more with less, and to do it faster.

The drama of those changes, and the necessity for them, is rooted in the popular sentiment in 1940. That year, twin currents collided at the center of America's national life. On the one hand, polls, editorials and interviews with average citizens all seemed to indicate that few people wanted to get mixed up in the expanding European mayhem. America was still shipping scrap metal to Japan. Hitler seemed to be a problem that the French and British would solve. The noninterventionist sentiment was summed up at one extreme in a poster from the America First Committee. The poster was headlined "War's First Casualty" and showed the Statue of Liberty's arm blown off by a rocket.

Although noninterventionists were outspoken and common, an opposite trend was also at work: rearmament and military preparedness. In September 1939, President Roosevelt had declared a state of "limited emergency." America wasn't really at war, but at the same time it was no longer at peace. Historians sometimes use the term *national defense period* to describe the years from 1939 to 1941. Groups such as the Committee to Defend America by Aiding the Allies crusaded for rapid military build-up. Military rearmament was popular in many areas of the country, because it

opened factories and produced jobs. Memories of the Depression were fresh and bitter, and anything that promised a regular paycheck was OK by most workers, whatever the state of international politics.

The newspaper headlines didn't seem to be cooperating with the nation's desire for neutrality. Soon folks were reading about what historian and author Allan Nevins (writing in the 1946 book *While You Were Gone*) called "the thunderclaps which shook men awake from their illusions." Combat ripped through Belgium, Flanders and the Sudan. The French armies collapsed. The Germans raced to the English Channel, forcing the British to evacuate 335,000 men through Dunkirk. War was apparently coming, and Americans were pitifully unprepared.

President Roosevelt was not a typical citizen, of course, and did far more than reflect the consensus. He never doubted that we would get into the war. At the end of summer in 1940, he ordered a general mobilization of the National Guard, along with the Navy and Marine reserves. He also asked Congress to pass the Selective Service Act, which was approved and signed into law in September, covering men ages twenty-one to thirty-five. It was the first American peacetime draft. In time, 16 million men would receive their registration cards, with the promise of earning $21 per month, should they be drafted into the Army as buck privates. More than 750,000 *selectees* (the wartime term for draftees) entered training by June 1941. The behemoth of American industry slowly and deliberately began converting to military production, mostly to help America's allies at the outset.

Even though FDR was certain which way the wind was blowing, the citizens and Congress remained reluctant to come to terms with the conflict. On May 21, 1941, a German U-boat torpedoed the American freighter *Robin Moor* in the South Atlantic, and still America refused to declare war, although it did step up the pace of preparation.

See Action Now

★ JOIN THE SUBMARINE SERVICE

This unsigned poster, from 1944, combines a striking illustration with a simple message. In fact, only a small percentage of all the people serving in the military saw direct action in combat; some sources put the figure as low as ten percent.

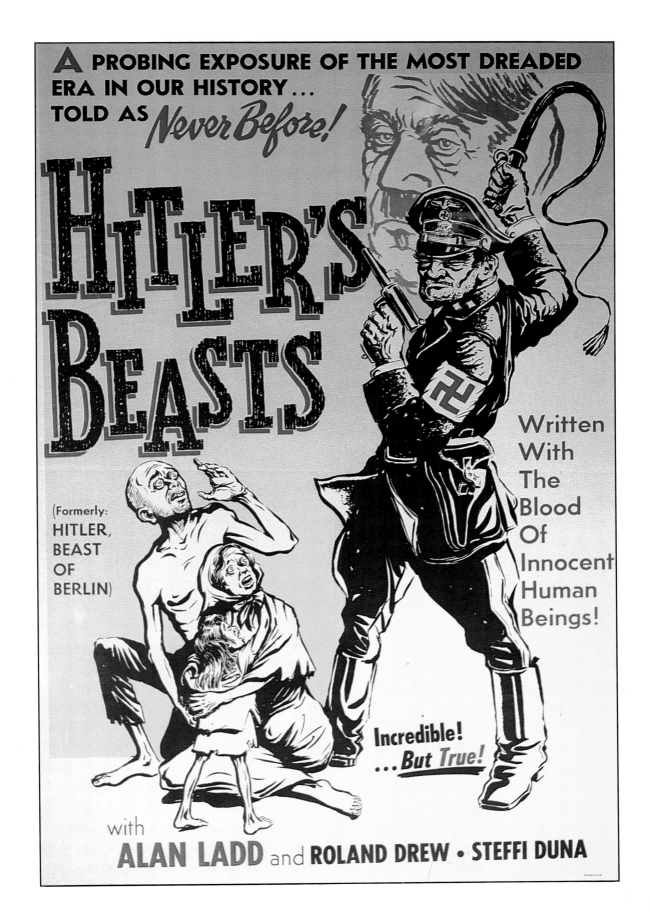

The war gradually worked its way into the expec-

Previous page
Although this film is not remembered as a fine effort of the war, the Hitler's Beasts *poster contains a memorable, gangsterish caricature of a Nazi and a tired, grim-looking Hitler.*

The war gradually worked its way into the expectations and the mental landscape of the average citizen. On the morning of Pearl Harbor, wrote Lee Kennett, in *For the Duration,* "in a nation still technically at peace, adventure and action lay in another war, the one waged against subversion. The theme was pervasive in that Sunday's [comic] strips: Don Winslow of the Navy was trying to ferret out a saboteur on board the USS Vermont [and] Tim Tyler pulled from the surf a half-drowned sailor who gasped the words 'foreign spy.'"

By October 1941, ten American merchant ships had been sunk, two warships attacked and more than 100 Americans killed. On December 7, 1941, Pearl Harbor decisively pushed the United States over the brink. News of the attack arrived at the Oakland Civic Center, where an America First rally was in progress. The assembly featured speaker Senator Gerald Nye of North Dakota, who had just spent two hours denouncing FDR as a warmonger. Nye was handed a note that described what had happened at Pearl Harbor; he read it to the audience. He said that he couldn't believe it.

On December 7, telephone lines around the United States were jammed. Some telephone companies ran spot announcements on the radio, asking people to stay off the lines so that important official calls could go through. One item in a book called *December 7, the First Thirty Hours* was a news report about the reaction

Not everyone could enlist in the military, but nevertheless plenty of jobs were available. Some people did their part by going to work, helping build what FDR called the arsenal of democracy in factories and on production lines. On the tiny end of the poster spectrum were small signs such as this one, here being mounted in a window by the wife of an Oldsmobile employee. Her husband may have been making artillery shells or cannon barrels. These signs were the civilian equivalent of the service flag. Oldsmobile History Center.

HOME OF A
SOLDIER OF
PRODUCTION
WE KEEP 'EM FIRING!

18

of the people in Birmingham, Alabama: "They are deeply resentful of the treachery. Vengeance-bent, confident of victory, dazzled by cataclysm, but with little second thought yet of the cost." Some recruiting stations opened that Sunday to handle the immediate ground swell of sentiment.

One month after Pearl Harbor, the Army announced it would double in size. The selective service system was picking up steam, funneling most draftees into the Army's ground forces, mainly the Infantry. An expanded draft law covering men ages twenty to forty-four was passed, setting February 15, 1942, as the registration date. Fellows in uniform were a common sight in every city and town, in every bus terminal and railroad station. Even before Pearl Harbor, and certainly by the end of 1941, "the reminders of the war were everywhere," veteran and writer Donald Rogers later wrote in *Since You Went Away*.

Posters blossomed on public buildings, urging first men and soon women to enlist. Through 1942, the Navy and Marines would get plenty of volunteers, as would the Army Air Forces (AAF), recognized early on as the most glamorous service. And the guys who signed up had plenty of famous and familiar examples to follow.

The war permeated the world of jobs and the headlines in the newspapers. It quickly reached into the gossip columns and the sports pages as well. Just as many Toms, Dicks and Harrys from small-town America went to war, so did the celebrities and sports heroes. Rogers recalled the significant enlistment of boxer Joe Louis. "Among all celebrities, even if you included the top movie stars, the politicians and radio personalities, Joe Louis was *the* hero to most Americans in 1941 and for a long time after that," Rogers wrote. When Louis went, folks knew things were getting mighty serious. Louis appeared on a well-known recruiting poster early in the war.

Ted Williams and Hank Greenberg also made headlines when they enlisted, although Greenberg would only serve six months. Professional baseball eventually sent 4,000 men into the service, carrying on its league playing schedule with the remaining 1,700. A less serious effect of the war was that night games were canceled sporadically, particularly in blackout-conscious coastal cities during 1943. Most baseball stars in the service were facing fastballs instead of bullets, however, as they served on morale-boosting, touring teams. But baseball was more than just a game, it was important; the War Department arranged to have the World Series games broadcast to the fighting fronts.

On the Hollywood scene, John Ford (who directed *The Informer* and *The Grapes of Wrath*) served as a commander in the Navy and made *The Battle of Midway*, a documentary, released in August 1942. The posters for the onslaught of war-related films made during the war could also have served as combination morale boosters and recruiting tools. When *The Shores of Tripoli* played in theaters around the United States, for example, Marine Corps recruiting booths appeared in the lobbies.

In the summer of 1941, the theater and film industry had been attacked by isolationists in Congress and in the press for "warmongering." Yet of all the films made in 1942, less than a third were related to the war, a ratio that continued throughout the conflict. Warner Brothers polled film viewers and found that most of them

The Division of Information of the Office for Emergency Management didn't waste any graphic resources on this poster from 1941. As a result, it is more of a broadside than a true poster. The federal government grudgingly came to grips with the problems of alerting the populace while not alarming it. In mid 1940, Secretary of War Harry Woodring wrote to President Roosevelt that he thought "an appeal to the public at this time for the organization of local defense committees would needlessly alarm our people and would tend to create the erroneous impression that the military forces of the nation are unprepared to deal with any likely threat to our security." That attitude was held by numerous government officials at all levels, until swept away by Pearl Harbor, the West Coast air raid scares and the flood of public sentiment to get involved.

voted for escapism and diversion.

One of John Ford's counterparts, Darryl Zanuck, was a lieutenant colonel. The top star of Zanuck's 20th Century-Fox studio was Betty Grable. In 1944, the *Motion Picture Herald* reported that she was the year's biggest box-office attraction. Just because she didn't enlist doesn't mean that she didn't do her part: she was a morale booster par excellence on the pinup front,

"A steady stream of tanks and planes"

Two days after Pearl Harbor, President Franklin Roosevelt sounded the themes with which Americans would become increasingly familiar during the war years: speed production, pull together, make sacrifices, get used to shortages, and cheerfully do your part. This excerpt is from Roosevelt's radio broadcast of December 9, 1941.

A year and a half has elapsed since the fall of France, when the whole world realized the mechanized might which the Axis nations had been building up for so many years. America has used that year and a half to great advantage. Knowing that the attack might reach us in all too short a time, we immediately began greatly to increase our industrial strength and our capacity to meet the demands of modern warfare.

Precious months were gained by sending vast quantities of our war material to the nations of the world still able to resist Axis aggression. Our policy rested on the fundamental truth that the defense of any country resisting Hitler or Japan was in the long run the defense of our own country. That policy has been justified. It has given us time, invaluable time, to build our American assembly lines of production.

Assembly lines are now in operation. Others are being rushed to completion. A steady stream of tanks and planes, of guns and ships, of shells and equipment—that is what these eighteen months have given us.

But it is all only a beginning of what still has to be done. We must be set to face a long war against crafty and powerful bandits. The attack at Pearl Harbor can be repeated at any one of many points in both oceans and along both our coast lines and against all the rest of the hemisphere.

It will not only be a long war, it will be a hard war. That is the basis on which we now lay all our plans. That is the yardstick by which we measure what we shall need and demand: money, materials, doubled and quadrupled production—ever increasing. The production must be not only for our own Army and Navy and Air Forces. It must reinforce the other armies and navies and air forces fighting the Nazis and the war lords of Japan throughout the Americas and the world.

I have been working today on the subject of production. Your Government has decided on two broad policies.

The first is to speed up all existing production by working on a seven-day-week basis in every war industry, including the production of essential raw materials.

The second policy, now being put into form, is to rush additions to the capacity of production by building more new plants, by adding to old plants, and by using the many smaller plants for war needs.

Over the hard road of the past months, we have at times met obstacles and difficulties, divisions and disputes, indifference and callousness. That is now all past—and, I am sure, forgotten.

The fact is that the country now has an organization in Washington built around men and women who are recognized experts in their own fields. I think the country knows that the people who are actually responsible in each and every one of these many fields are pulling together with a teamwork that has never before been excelled.

On the road ahead there lies hard work—grueling work—day and night, every hour and every minute.

I was about to add that ahead there lies sacrifice for all of us.

But it is not correct to use that word. The United States does not consider it a sacrifice to do all one can, to give one's best to our nation, when the nation is fighting for its existence and its future life.

It is not a sacrifice for any man, old or young, to be in the Army or the Navy of the United States. Rather it is a privilege.

It is not a sacrifice for the industrialist or the wage-earner, the farmer or the shopkeeper, the trainman or the doctor, to pay more taxes, to buy more bonds, to forego extra profits, to work longer or harder at the task for which he is best fitted. Rather it is a privilege.

It is not a sacrifice to do without many things to which we are accustomed if the national defense calls for doing without.

A review this morning leads me to the conclusion that at present we shall not have to curtail the normal use of articles of food. There is enough food today for all of us and enough left over to send to those who are fighting on the same side with us.

But there will be a clear and definite shortage of metals of many kinds for civilian use, for the very good reason that in our increased program we shall need for war purposes more than half of that portion of the principal metals which during the past year have gone into articles for civilian use. We shall have to give up many things entirely.

I am sure that the people in every part of the nation are prepared in their individual living to win this war. I am sure they will cheerfully help to pay a large part of its financial cost while it goes on. I am sure they will cheerfully give up those material things they are asked to give up.

I am sure that they will retain all those great spiritual things without which we cannot win through.

brightening thousands of barracks walls and fueling millions of GI fantasies.

Other Hollywood stars joined the ranks, as well. Ginger Rogers married a Marine private, Dorothy Lamour married an AAF captain. Henry Fonda, Mickey Rooney and Gene Autry made up a prominent trio. And Clark Gable went in the Air Force, along with Jimmy Stewart and Glenn Miller.

By 1944, Jimmy Stewart was a major, had been pilot-commander of a dozen missions over Germany and had earned a Distinguished Flying Cross for a raid on aircraft factories in Brunswick, Germany, in which twenty US planes had been shot down. Clark Gable had

also seen true-life action. Even before that, he'd had a unique, ringside seat on the war when President Roosevelt made his fifteenth fireside chat, just after New Year in 1941. The speech would become a famous and much-

Next page
Compared with many of the realistic, detailed posters from World War II *that depicted vivid battle scenes and graphic combat, this 1942 poster seems more like a World War I effort because of the uniform. Nevertheless, the uniform depicted was the official one at the outset of the war; the more familiar M1 steel helmet and field jacket didn't appear until 1943.*

William Young, publisher of the Record-Express *in Lititz, Pennsylvania, also did triple duty as a reporter and advertising representative during the war. The service star—propped behind him on the shelf—indicates that one of his four*

employees was already in the service. Marjory Collins made this photo for the Office of War Information in November 1942. Library of Congress.

quoted edition, in which FDR announced that America "must be the great arsenal of democracy." It was broadcast to 500 radio stations. Witnesses to the talk, in the small Oval Room at the White House, were FDR's mother, the secretary of state—and Clark Gable.

At various times and to various degrees, the folks at home felt a catalog of emotions; foremost were anger, fear, determination and confusion. This welter of anxiety and activity had been anticipated by the government, which had created the Office of Civilian Defense

In New York, an Italian-American shoemaker is on duty as an air raid warden at sector headquarters on Waverly Place. This *photo was made by Marjory Collins in December 1942 for the Office of War Information.* Library of Congress.

(OCD) in May 1941. The OCD's main task was to coordinate local organizations, which was very difficult. Even simple supplies were hard to get; air-raid wardens lacked arm bands and whistles. "Of gas masks—for many people the tangible symbol of 'protection'—there were simply none," Lee Kennett wrote. There was also a nationwide shortage of air-raid sirens, which were in any event hard to hear and which many people couldn't interpret if they did hear one.

The OCD issued an air-raid pamphlet the day after Pearl Harbor but still needed a clear, easy-to-read set of instructions about what to do during an air raid. Cartoonist Milt Caniff had been asked to do one several weeks earlier. Right after Pearl Harbor, he went to Washington with his letterer, meeting with staff members from the OCD and the Chemical Warfare Service. They got the project done quickly and rushed it to the Government Printing Office as a top priority, and the first copies were airlifted to the West Coast. Within a week, Caniff's work appeared as a full-page spread in hundreds of newspapers. Boy Scouts distributed the poster nationwide.

Another result of Pearl Harbor seems minor in retrospect but offers insight into the temperament and mood of the times. Residents of the West Coast became temporarily terrorized about the possibility of Japanese attacks, anticipating such targets as the Navy Yard at Puget Sound, the Boeing plant in Seattle, the Douglas and North American Aviation plants at Santa Monica, and the Douglas plant at Long Beach. A frenzy of local interest in civil defense followed.

Bombers seemed to be a real menace to Americans in 1942; a Gallup poll in December 1941 found that half the United States expected air attacks.

Once the air-raid wardens got on the case, false alarms were common, Kennett wrote, "traceable for the most part to overzealous and inexperienced aerial observers, or to radar operators who misinterpreted the idiosyncracies" of their equipment. For example, on December 9, 1941, aviators reported sighting thirty-four Japanese warships between San Francisco and Los Angeles. The warships turned out to be fourteen domestic fishing boats.

Although attacks did not come from above, the residents' worries weren't entirely groundless. Japanese submarines made several attacks on West Coast tankers and freighters.

Another menace quickly assumed gigantic proportions: the concern with espionage and sabotage. It would prove much more durable than the threat of Japanese aircraft and would serve as the inspiration for dozens of posters throughout the war. Looking at the forbidding posters, peopled with nightmarish images of enemy subversives, one would think spies were at every bus stop and bar. People were afraid that radio broadcasts might contain secret, coded messages, so radio stations dropped man-in-the-street interviews and programs where callers could request songs.

Most historians now seem skeptical about the extent and success of actual espionage efforts during the war. "In the end this enemy [foreign espionage] proved to be as much of a phantom as the Japanese airplanes which glimmered on the radar screens of the Western Defense Command," wrote Kennett. As early as 1942, one observer had realized that "the black-outs and dimouts, the air raid drills, the boxes of sand and the pails of water are the remnants of a gigantic false alarm."

At various times, the federal planners and observers were baffled. After Pearl Harbor, they expected mobs of people to panic, and sometimes seemed surprised that the panic didn't occur. If people sounded the air-raid siren too often, they seemed to be overreacting. However, if they didn't act worried, they seemed to be complacent.

Nevertheless, like so many other aspects of the war, initial hesitation and confusion were followed by extraordinary activity and achievement. By the summer of 1942, the OCD had some 10 million volunteers, active in every phase of the home front effort. Apart from organizing civil defense, the OCD also helped mobilize salvage drives for rubber, tin, aluminum and paper, and sales of war bonds. The volunteers channeled the energy of the folks at home, diverting them into tangible projects that helped people feel that they were doing their part in the larger effort.

HELP BRING THEM BACK TO YOU!

THIS IS A V HOME

Find time for war work

Raise and share food

Walk and carry packages

Conserve everything you have

Save 10% in War Bonds

MAKE YOURS A VICTORY HOME!

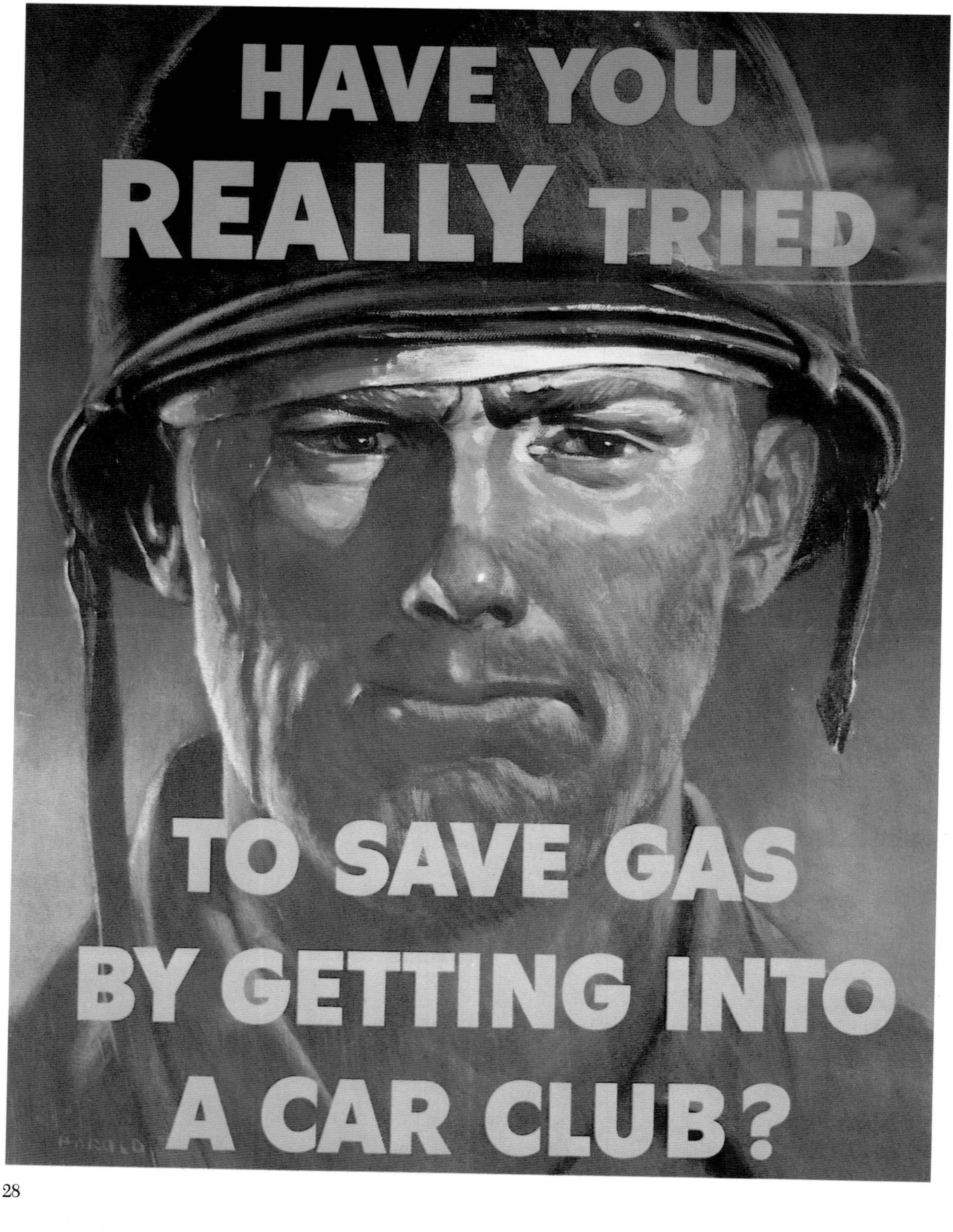
HAVE YOU
REALLY TRIED
TO SAVE GAS
BY GETTING INTO
A CAR CLUB?

Chapter 2

Rationing and Conservation

"Suddenly the Good American Was Told to Do Without"

Doing without movie stars and sports heroes was a trivial deprivation of the war. The shortages and rationing encountered at stores seemed more intimate. There was always another handsome actor, but there weren't any more tennis shoes or dozens of other familiar things. Many of the shortages figured into posters, which either mentioned a product or commodity directly or encouraged participation in dozens of conservation measures and salvage campaigns.

Early in the war, the Consumer Division of the Office of Price Administration produced a small, mail-in card entitled "The Consumer's Victory Pledge." It said, "As a consumer, in the total defense of democracy, I will do my part to make my home, my community, my country ready, efficient and strong.

"I will buy carefully.

"I will take good care of the things I have.

"I will waste nothing . . ."

The "waste nothing" motif featured in dozens of posters.

As early as the summer of 1941, the Office of Price Administration was sure that rationing would be necessary. Hints and more tangible evidence were not long in reaching the average consumer. In late 1941, the shiny chrome bumpers disappeared from the 1942 model cars, in some cases replaced by bumpers painted yellow. The last cars rolled off the assembly lines in mid-February of 1942, and the dwindling stock of new autos was rationed to doctors, veterinarians, clergy and public officials.

In the spring of 1942, the first gas shortages hit the East Coast. That March, U-boats sunk a score of tankers

Previous page
For a people who loved automobiles and who enjoyed just going out for a weekend drive to nowhere, the answer to this question didn't come easy. If they were asked the question today, almost fifty years later, most Americans would have to answer no.

Millions of American consumers either took the pledge or felt guilty if they didn't. Although black markets cropped up during the war, they were sporadic and generally insignificant. National Archives.

along the lower East Coast and in the Gulf of Mexico. In the first six months of the year, that total climbed to more than 200 tankers. By mid-May, 8.4 million motorists in the coastal states had registered for gas-rationing cards. "It was as though the enemy had found a particularly vulnerable place to strike—the sacred bond which united the American and his car," Lee Kennett wrote in *For the Duration*. "For the owner of a twelve-cylinder Packard and a three-gallon-a-week ration card, the war became the grimmest of realities."

"Pleasure" driving of any kind was out. Motorists received windshield stickers, lettered A through E. *A* was for driving considered nonessential to the war. Holders of A-stickers originally drew 5 gallons per week. Later they drew 4 gallons per week, then 3, which was equivalent to about 60 miles of driving. *B* was for people who commuted to work but didn't use their vehicle on the job. *C* was for salespeople and

delivery people, and E was for emergency workers—police, firefighters, clergy, press photographers and reporters. The presence of the last two categories on the E-list testifies to the importance placed on news gathering during the war.

Folks coped in a number of ways: sharing rides, riding bicycles or simply not going. A corny Hollywood publicity photo illustrates how a "Hollywood actress" got by with 3 gallons per week. It shows her at the wheel, looking at a small chart attached to the dashboard. The chart says things like, "Monday—1 gal. to studio and back," "Thursday—½ gal. to Bond Rally," and "Friday—½ gal. to location trip."

"Me travel? . . . not this summer," announces the citizen in a poster by Albert Dorne, done for the Department of Defense Transportation in 1945. "Vacation at home," the poster suggests. It shows a man in an easy chair, smoking a pipe, reading the newspaper,

Metal took on versatile properties on war posters, especially in the hands of copywriters who could ignore all the intervening steps of the salvage process—collection, smelting, refining and finally recasting into weapons—and go right from *frying pan to bombshell in one easy slogan. This Army poster is from 1943; the artist's name is illegible. Note that one crew member wears an Army cartridge belt, perhaps because this poster was issued by the Army.*

sipping an iced drink, with a fan blowing on him. A serviceman's picture is on a shelf.

In March of 1942, serious measures were proposed in Congress to conserve the tires on the United States' 30 million cars and 5 million trucks. They included a reduction in the national speed limit to 40 mph or even 35 mph, increased gas rationing and scrap rubber collection. The few new tires that were available were reserved for trucks that hauled essential materials; you could get tires for your truck if you used it to carry beehives but not if you used it to carry beer or juke boxes.

Once the plea went out nationwide for help with the rubber shortage, the government received 8,000 letters containing ideas for conserving or reclaiming rubber. Ads, posters and even radio shows spread the word. Writer Don Quinn, who scripted the popular radio comedy *Fibber McGee and Molly*, included the

theme of tire conservation—as well as themes such as the shortage of nurses and other concerns—in the show's story line.

On April 27, sugar rationing began with the distribution of War Ration Book Number One, the "Sugar Book," containing twenty-eight folded stamps. A million teachers at America's schools doled out the booklets, each containing a year's supply of coupons for sugar purchases. In all, they issued 122 million ration books and coupon booklets.

In May, the War Production Board (WPB) issued Order M–126, which halted production of 400 civilian products that used steel or iron. Coupons were eventually issued, at various times, for butter, cheese, canned goods and meat, forcing shoppers to begin trying to remember ceiling prices and figure out "points." (Goods were assigned point values, with scarce or desirable items having higher values.) One researcher counted fifteen "essential commodities" that were ultimately rationed in the United States.

The government went to great lengths to explain to consumers why some types of food were in short

Gas rationing, the lack of new cars, shortages of tires and auto mechanics, workers moving to the site of new industries—all these things combined to put unprecedented demands on trains and buses. The Office of Defense Transportation issued OWI poster number 74 in 1943, in an effort to free as many seats as possible for soldiers who were reporting for training or making final visits home.

Rationing was new to most Americans; its bureaucracy and procedures took some explaining. National Archives.

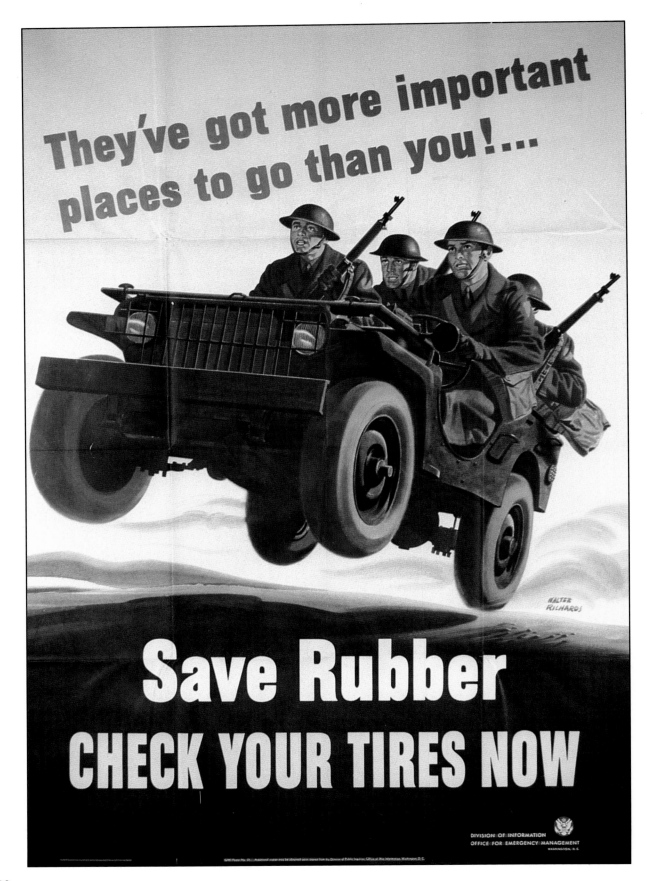

Previous page
The image of a jeep no doubt struck a responsive chord among viewers of this poster. The vehicle was popular among soldiers and civilians alike, picking up nicknames such as blitzbuggy, iron pony and jitterbug. Scientific American magazine in January 1942 ran an article called "Meet the Jeep, the United States Army's Answer to Schickelgruber's Panzer Divisions." Walter Richards made this poster in 1942; it was OWI poster number 21, produced for the Division of Information, Office for Emergency Management.

supply and where the food was going (to the troops, of course). The government agencies used posters, and films as well. Walt Disney's second wartime film was a short called *Food Will Win the War,* produced for the Agriculture Department and paid for by the Office of Strategic Services, which, in June 1942, was one of several agencies unified in the Office of War Information. Disney next made *Out of the Frying Pan into the Firing Line,* an incentive film for the Conservation Di-

A familiar scene during the war: standing in line at the local rationing board, which has signs extending down the length of this block in New Orleans, Louisiana. Clearly, soldiers weren't exempt. John Vachon made this photo for the Office of War Information in March 1943. Library of Congress.

34

Most Americans needed little encouragement to dig up a garden plot and plant a few tomatoes. Many folks were doing it anyway, and the added overtone of patriotism made those fresh vegetables taste even better. National Archives.

vision of the War Production Board. That encouraged housewives to save kitchen fat and grease. This film augmented the message of several wartime posters. One of them shows a hand holding a frying pan and pouring grease into a cluster of bombs and torpedoes, which seem to be flying outward toward the viewer. "Save waste fats for explosives. Take them to your meat dealer," the poster says. It was painted by H. Koerner for the Office of War Information in 1943.

The film industry itself wasn't exempt from shortages, of course. Hollywood experienced shortages of film, as well as of blank cartridges for Westerns. Elsewhere in the media, phonograph record production

Previous page
The notion of making military airplanes out of wood, as indicated in this 1943 poster, seems odd today. Nevertheless, training planes were made from wood, as were the gliders that played a crucial role in the invasion of D-day, then flown by England's Ox and Bucks (Oxfordshire and Buckinghamshire) regiment.

Next page
Although few documented shortages of fresh vegetables occurred during the war, Americans gardened with a vengeance—to such an extent that the Department of Agriculture, which had campaigned against first-time, urban victory gardens early in the war, changed its tune and proclaimed them both necessary and patriotic. This version, from 1943, was OWI poster number 34.

FOOD FOR FREEDOM

Produce more MILK for HIM

UNITED STATES DEPARTMENT OF AGRICULTURE

WAR BOARDS

was cut seventy percent and paper allotments twenty-five percent. The effect of this last measure on the publishing industry was profound and would last throughout the war.

A March 1945 edition of Raymond Chandler's *Farewell My Lovely* has this inscription:

Books in Wartime
"Books are weapons in the war of ideas."
—President Roosevelt

This book is manufactured in compliance with the War Production Board's ruling for conserving paper.

It is printed on lighter weight paper, which reduces bulk substantially, and has smaller margins with more words to each page. The text is complete and unabridged.

Thinner and smaller books will not only save paper, plate metal and man power, but will make more books available to the reading public.

The reader's understanding of this wartime problem will enable the publisher to cooperate more fully with our Government.

By June 1942, the following items were no longer being produced: cars, trucks, metal office furniture, radios, phonographs, electric refrigerators, vacuum cleaners, washing machines and sewing machines. That

Like James Montgomery Flagg's "You can lick runaway prices" poster, this one was done for the Office of Economic Stabilization's Seven Keys to Victory campaign. All seven tactics are things that a private citizen on the home front could do. The palm trees suggest an island in the Pacific, the hot venue late in the war.

The place is West Danville, Vermont. The date is July 1942. The paperwork explosion that accompanied the bombs and artillery of the war makes itself felt at Hastings' General Store. "You can't carry on a business, especially nowadays, without a lot of book work," Hastings told the photographer. "But whether it is for income tax or making up price lists for cost-of-living commodities, it is all a part of keeping our government going so we can win the war and have the kind of world we want." Controlled products included milk, cream, ice cream, canned goods, bananas, frozen vegetables and fruits, beef and pork, peanuts, soups, paper, coffee, tea and tobacco. Products not controlled included butter, cheese, condensed milk, fresh fruit and vegetables, flour, mutton and lamb, fresh fish, nuts, prunes, dry beans, eggs and poultry. Fritz Henle made this photo for the Office of War Information. Library of Congress.

"More money than has ever been spent by any nation"

In this radio broadcast of April 28, 1942, President Franklin Roosevelt tries to explain a few facts about skyrocketing spending by the government. He makes price controls sound like a spontaneous, patriotic duty, but the government issued stringent laws, as well.

Not all of us can have the privilege of fighting our enemies in distant parts of the world.

Not all of us can have the privilege of working in a munitions factory or shipyard, or on the farms or in oil fields or mines, producing the weapons or the raw materials which are needed by our armed forces.

But there is one front and one battle where everyone in the United States—every man, woman, and child—is in action and will be privileged to remain in action throughout this war. That front is right here at home, in our daily lives and in our daily tasks. Here at home everyone will have the privilege of making whatever self-denial is necessary, not only to supply our fighting men, but to keep the economic structure of our country fortified and secure during the war and after the war.

This will require the abandonment not only of luxuries but many other creature comforts.

Every loyal American is aware of his individual responsibility. Whenever I hear anyone saying, "The American people are complacent—they need to be aroused," I feel like asking him to come to Washington and read the mail that floods into the White House and into all departments of this Government.

The one question that recurs through all these thousands of letters and messages is: "What more can I do to help my country in winning this war?"

To build factories, and buy the materials, and pay the labor, and provide the transportation, and equip and feed and house the soldiers, sailors, and marines, and to do all the thousands of things necessary in a war—all cost money, more money than has ever been spent by any nation at any time in the history of the world.

We are now spending, solely for war purposes, the sum of about $100,000,000 every day in the week. But before this year is over, that almost unbelievable rate of expenditure will be doubled.

All of this money has to be spent—and spent quickly—if we are to produce within the time now available the enormous quantities of weapons of war which we need. But the spending of these tremendous sums presents grave danger of disaster to our national economy.

When your Government continues to spend these unprecedented sums for munitions month by month and year by year, that money goes into the pocketbooks and bank accounts of the people of the United States. At the same time raw materials and many manufactured goods are necessarily taken away from civilian use; and machinery and factories are being converted to war production.

You do not have to be a professor of economics to see that if people with plenty of cash start bidding against each other for scarce goods the price of them goes up.

---

summer, shoppers noticed shortages of cosmetics, hairpins, tinfoil and alcohol. After September, no irons, water heaters, lawn mowers, waffle irons, toasters, percolators and food mixers were produced in the United States.

Congress's response was typical. It created yet another agency in the alphabet-soup style of the times, the Office of Price Administration (OPA), to fix retail and wholesale prices as a guard against inflation and price gouging, to ration scarce items, and to hold down wages and rents. The OPA's legal mechanisms were the General Maximum Price Regulation—which froze almost all manufacturing, wholesale and retail prices, but which didn't include wages or the price of farm items—and the Supplementary Price Control Act, enacted in October 1942. Prices rose only slightly during the next two years. For comparison, in England, the average weekly wage rose eighty percent during the war and the cost of living rose thirty-one percent.

American citizens were urged to save more and buy less, and to pay off their debts. It was an unfamiliar message. During the brief splurge after the Depression, the consumer had been urged to buy everything new "by advertisements which shouted at him from newspapers, magazines, and billboards" wrote Henry Pringle in *While You Were Gone*. "Suddenly the good American was told to do without; to patch, mend, and save." Many posters tied conservation of scarce products directly to patriotism.

Actually, the theme of "make do with less" wasn't a creation of World War II. During World War I, the US Food Administration produced a poster that said, "Blood or bread—others are giving their blood. You will shorten the war [and] save life if you eat only what you need, and waste nothing." In 1943, the Office of War Information struck the same chord with a poster that exhorted, "Do with less—so they'll have enough! Rationing gives you your fair share."

Americans could take some comfort in knowing that it wasn't nearly as bad in the United States as it was in England. According to writer Denis Judd, author of

Next page
The OWI issued this pep talk for rationing in 1943. The soldier's expression puts him firmly in the "war isn't so bad, after all" school of combat art.

40

Previous page
R. Couillard's message in this 1943 poster is clear: Don't complain about having to fork over some of your paycheck for taxes or having to carry a book of ration tickets—it beats getting bombed. War is hell, but it is more hellish in some places than in others. The War Finance Division of the Treasury Department issued this poster.

Posters of World War II, compared with the British and Russians, Americans "suffered little deprivation." In England, rationing began in January 1940 and didn't end entirely until nine years after the war, in 1954. Onions became so rare that they were used as prizes at raffles and treasure hunts. In Russia, food rationing was severe; bread was rationed on the basis of the work someone did, with office workers getting half as much as industrial workers.

Wartime shortages helped spur a national return to America's agrarian roots in the form of victory gardens, which cropped up even in the vacant lots of New York and Chicago. According to some estimates, one fourth of the American urban population, and a larger proportion of country dwellers, grew millions of bushels of vegetables and fruit in 1944. One victory gardener in New Orleans grew 30 pounds of tomatoes, 100 ears of corn, radishes, lettuce and cabbage in an empty downtown parking lot. In England, Potato Pete and Dr. Carrot encouraged homegrown foods in posters and advertisements.

Today, people tend to assume that the victory garden phenomenon always had official support, but that isn't quite the way it was. The US Department of Agriculture (USDA), in a November 1941 press release, had in fact warned against "emergency" or "defense" gardens, because American farmers were producing

Next page
This foreign relief poster, since it dealt with compassion, was the opposite of the posters that emphasized hate and revenge. By 1944, when this poster was issued, war victims included orphaned children, refugees, widows, wounded soldiers and civilians in dozens of countries.

"Grow your own and play safe"

The Office of War Information was a cornucopia of data, issuing it in a barrage of pep talks, guides and manuals. In this letter, a staff member at OWI headquarters in Washington relays information to the branch that designed most of the posters.

Office of War Information
Washington

January 26, 1945

Mr. James D. Herbert
New York Art Director
Bureau of Graphics
Office of War Information
250 West 57th Street
New York 19, New York

Dear Mr. Herbert:

The fact sheet on Victory Gardens was not available as soon as I thought it would be, and, therefore, the delay in getting information on this program to you.

The salient facts on this program are:

Farmers are suffering from lack of manpower, as much or more than any other group. It is unlikely that they could continue to produce vegetables as they did in 1944 without a decrease in the production of the other essential foods.

These are the production figures. In 1944, farmers harvested vegetables from 3,924,000 acres. In 1945 their goal is to plant only 3,838,000 acres—a decrease of 86,000 acres.

With the increasing number of fighting men overseas and on ships, more and more canned vegetables must be shipped to them. They must be served first. Last year our fighting forces received 41% of all the canned vegetables we produced. This year they will require a still greater quantity. Victory gardeners are called upon to make up the shortage—for their country's sake and for their own.

Appeals to Victory Gardeners in 1945
1. *Garden for Victory*
   Gardens that supply 40% of our fresh vegetables are essential to win the war.
2. *Grow Your Own and Play Safe*
   If you have your own fruits and vegetables, you don't have to worry about crop failures in other parts of the country.
3. *Save Money*
4. *Build Your Health*

Gardeners can obtain local advice and assistance from their V-G leaders, including county agents, garden clubs and committees. State information is available from the State Agricultural Colleges and Extension Services. Information also available from the U. S. Dept. of Agriculture in Washington, D. C.

Sincerely yours,

Gertrude E. Schwarz

Gertrude Schwarz

THEY NEED FOOD

Plant MORE BEANS

HELP FEED THOSE FREED FROM AXIS RULE

43

plenty, and more efficiently than backyard gardens could. However, the home folks hauled out the hoes and seed packets just the same. On December 20, 1941, the USDA's National Victory Garden Program targeted gardens in farms and villages, but cautioned people against plowing up their backyards and local parks. In February, the USDA again tried to discourage novice gardeners and folks who lived in large cities; these people could find other activities that might be more helpful to winning the war.

Writing in *America Organizes to Win the War* in 1942, Claude Wickard, secretary of agriculture, said, "It is the hope of the Department of Agriculture that 1.3 million more farm families will plant home vegetable gardens in 1942." Note that he specified "farm families." He continued, "There is nothing in the food-supply situation to warrant a hysterical campaign for city home gardens, which might result in plowing up lawns, parks, and athletic fields for growing vegetables."

However, official plans and pronouncements to the contrary, it was impossible to stop the gardens from proliferating. An Office of War Information poster in 1943 showed a cute daughter asking her mother, "We'll have lots to eat this winter, won't we mother?" The poster exhorted, "Grow your own, can your own." The mother in the illustration is twisting the lid onto a jar of beans; a shelf filled with other canned goods is behind them.

Once again, precedents were set back in World War I, when the government created the National War Garden Commission. One 1918 poster from this agency said, "Can vegetables, fruit and the Kaiser too." Like those in the Second World War, posters from World War I tied in whatever theme was current with combat. If rivet guns were like machine guns, then peas were like bullets. "Food is ammunition—don't waste it," commanded a poster by J. F. Sheridan for the US Food Administration.

A huge increase occurred in home canning, evidenced by articles such as one titled "Food Garden" in the March 27, 1944, issue of *Life*. It was a large drawing that promised, "This chart will help you grow 16 vegetables." Millions of meat-and-spuds Americans got a chance to try some new vegetables, cooked in new ways. Another wartime trend, however, was opposite of the home planted and home cooked: more people began to use store-bought breads and cereals, which were being fortified with vitamins A and D.

On the whole, citizens learned to take shortages and rationing in good stride, once they got used to them. "Since bitching and griping are not by any means an army monopoly, we squawked and complained and beefed about our growing shortages but, in the main, behaved better about them," Paul Gallico wrote in *While You Were Gone*, which was published just after the war. Certainly the inhabitants of posters did.

Jobs were plentiful and wages were high during the war. As a result, folks found out that they'd have to stand in lines everywhere—at barbershops, bars and movie theaters. When servicemen wrote home complaining about standing in line, their letters found an

HOW TO PREVENT INFLATION

WE CAN HELP PREVENT SKYROCKETING FOOD COSTS IF......

1. The grocer posts his Ceiling Price List and charges only ceilings or less.

2. The buyer uses the list—learns the proper prices—and pays no more.

3. The buyer doesn't hesitate to call the grocer's attention to mistakes.

I'M ANXIOUS TO CORRECT ANY WRONG PRICES. SO ASK ME ABOUT THEM!

We don't want sky-high prices after this war! Remember that almost half of the total rise in prices during World War I took place AFTER THE ARMISTICE!

This need not happen again. Patriotic grocers are posting their Ceiling Price Lists . . . charging only ceilings or less . . . welcoming questions about prices. Patriotic buyers are using the lists . . . paying no more . . . asking friendly questions about possible mistakes. Are you doing your share . . . for the sake of America's future?

Co-operate with your grocer.
Know Ceiling Price Lists—pay no more!

This Advertising Space Has Been Donated To The

OFFICE OF PRICE ADMINISTRATION
Washington, D. C. by

NAME OF NEWSPAPER

This informative, public-service ad illustrates how the Office of War Information functioned as a middleman between client agencies (in this case, the Office of Price Administration) and the civilian media. OWI provided the camera-ready copy, and a local newspaper inserted its name at the bottom. National Archives.

Next page
McClelland Barclay, who was in the Naval Reserve, did this poster in 1941 or 1942 for the Salvage Division of the War Production Board. Barclay had produced prize-winning posters for the Navy back during World War I, when he was a member of the Committee on National Preparedness. He died in 1943. Note the plummeting aircraft in the background, poster shorthand for a battle victory.

SAVE YOUR CANS

Help pass the Ammunition

M?CLELLAND BARCLAY USNR

PREPARE YOUR TIN CANS
FOR WAR

1 REMOVE TOPS AND BOTTOMS
2 TAKE OFF PAPER LABELS
3 WASH THOROUGHLY
4 FLATTEN FIRMLY

Previous page
Just as industrial workers were encouraged to picture their contributions to combat, so were the folks who participated in salvage and conservation drives. Warren Baumgartner did this poster in 1942.

understanding audience. In numerous surveys, housewives reported that they, too, were tired of standing in line.

Small, sporadic black markets for gasoline, nylon stockings and meat persisted through the war years. Prohibition created bootleggers and speakeasies; during the war, shady cab drivers steered customers to a gas station that sold illegal ration coupons or a butcher who sold steaks at illegally high prices, no coupons asked. Instead of printing money, counterfeiters printed coupons.

The black market was just one hazard facing the war effort, and one of several focuses of government concern. According to D'Ann Campbell in *Women at War with America*, "on the whole, compliance was excellent and rationing worked as it was intended." On the other hand, in 1944, an OPA investigation of thousands of businesses revealed that more than half were violating price controls.

In 1944, a poster from the Government Printing Office returned to the "consumer's pledge" theme, but this time it spelled out two ways to cheat the system. "Keep the home front pledge," it said. "Pay no more than ceiling prices. Pay your points in full." With wages rising rapidly, shoppers often had more money than choices. Encouraging cheerful compliance with the rationing rules was a recurrent theme sounded in posters throughout the war.

The flip side of shortages and rationing was the tremendous drives to conserve goods and to turn in scrap materials. These drives gave the folks at home ways in which to do their part. The Office of Civilian Defense, created in May 1941, organized salvage drives for rubber, tin, paper and aluminum. The Boy Scouts alone salvaged 150,000 tons of paper by 1942. The OCD also encouraged first aid training and sponsored air raid drills. The War Production Board also had a Salvage Division, and its representatives became regular figures at the 20,000 automobile junkyards in the United States. Salvage operations eventually reached into factories, schools and prisons. In the year beginning February 1, 1942, more than a million junk cars were reclaimed from auto graveyards. Workers tore up abandoned railroads and street car tracks, bridges, oil wells and sunken vessels, in all cases looking for usable steel.

The drives to recover scrap metal and wastepaper from homes and farms involved millions of Americans, who were in turn informed and motivated in part by media campaigns. "The success of this extremely complicated and difficult operation could not have been so great without the wholehearted cooperation of the press, the radio, and the movies," wrote Donald Nelson,

head of the War Production Board, in his memoir *Arsenal of Democracy*.

Famous names also aided the cause. Eddie Rickenbacker spent twenty-four days on a raft after the pilot of his aircraft ditched in the Pacific in October 1942. In an interview in Life magazine, the famous aviator sent a message to the folks back home: "If only people knew that the saving of one old rubber tire makes it possible to produce one of these rafts, they might not worry whether they have their automobiles on weekends."

In the month that Rickenbacker briefly disappeared and was feared lost, American distillers had been forbidden to make drinking liquor; alcohol was needed for explosives. In early 1944, however, a couple experimental types of booze made from surplus potatoes were authorized. In June 1944, the WPB said distillers could resume production of neutral spirits for blending rye and bourbon.

In the fall of 1944, meats, fats and canned vegetables were briefly taken off rationing. However, in 1945, the Office of Price Administration announced that those goods were back on the list. Cigarettes were never rationed during the war, but, Donald Rogers wrote in *Since You Went Away*, "simply did not exist" from November 1944 through June 1945.

In 1945, shoppers also dealt with shortages of liquor, eggs, radios, coal, fuel and auto parts. This last insufficiency was especially vexing, since commuters and mechanics were dealing with increasingly beat-up cars.

A recurrent theme of poster and ad campaigns was the effort to convince folks at home not to hoard items that were scarce. In 1945, newspaper readers around the United States were pleased to hear the tale of a "lady hoarder" who had crammed her cellar with

Next page
Norman Rockwell produced OWI poster number 45 in 1943. This poster stirred up resentment because it seemed to portray America as a land of plenty when refugees in other countries were starving. Its well-known image is part of the "Ours to fight for" series, which included "Freedom from fear," "Freedom of speech" and "Freedom of worship." The story behind this series of posters has much to say about the workings of bureaucracy. When the war started, Rockwell and another illustrator, Mead Schaeffer, visited Washington with sketches of posters they were anxious to contribute. Rockwell's concept was to illustrate FDR's Four Freedoms, but he was rebuffed—by the Office of War Information, among others—in some cases because he was only an "illustrator," not an artist. He stopped in Philadelphia to present some covers he'd done for the Saturday Evening Post, *and the magazine commissioned him to follow through on his idea. When the magazine published the illustrations, it was deluged with requests for reprints. According to Philip Meggs, "The series achieved an iconic presence. Roosevelt's conceptualization was transformed into the reality of everyday life. . . . Needless to say, among the numerous federal agencies which reproduced 'The Four Freedoms' thousands of times in posters and publications was the Office of War Information."*

OURS...to fight for

FREEDOM FROM WANT

canned goods, only to have a flood wash off all the labels, making her canned meals a lottery for the duration.

On the whole, the experience of the citizen who stayed home during the war was mixed. Clearly, conditions were worse than before the war. "Whether describing housing, appliances, medical care, laundry, clothing or food, the story was much the same: inflation of work loads, hidden price increases as shoddy goods replaced durable items, shortages of amenities and necessities, and deterioration of the overall quality of life," D'Ann Campbell wrote.

At the same time, things could have been much worse. Although shortages were chronic throughout the war, an editorial in *Life* in January 1944 put the situation in perspective: "The U.S. remains, in the midst of war, a land of abundance," it said. "Washington is now busy with semi-secret plans for the reconversion of some portion of industry to civilian production." Bobby pins were on their way back into production, the article said, and 2 million electric irons were scheduled to be produced in 1944.

In general, the civilian production spigots were turned on again after V-E Day and V-J Day, sometimes with startling rapidity. Planners in the government and industry had done an excellent job anticipating the return to normal life. Butchers' cases were soon full, and stacks of tires appeared at garages. You could fill up your car easily and cruise down to buy a new pair of shoes.

After forty-three months of restrictions, the War Production Board told car makers they could make all the automobiles they wished. The WPB also promptly lifted the curbs on electric dishwashers, washing machines, electric shavers, pots and pans, radios, film, batteries, toys, paper napkins, suits, shoes, phonographs, records, cameras, garden tools and shop tools. "Starting in 1945, the consumers' astonishing appetite for food, clothing, housing, cars, household equipment, and leisure gear has set off the wildest buying spree in U.S. history, or for that matter, in the world," wrote Joseph Seldin, author of *The Golden Fleece*.

There was also the matter of $90 billion worth of military surplus goods left over from the war: $50 million worth of 60 inch searchlights, for example, and 40,000 surplus homing pigeons. But no one had much time to worry about them; most of the 12 million American soldiers and sailors—human homing pigeons wearing uniforms and medals—were on their way back from Europe and the Pacific.

This display includes everything that wasn't for sale during wartime Christmas. Shoppers could drool, but the message was, "Why not give a war bond instead?" National Archives.

Chapter 3

Industrial Production

A Struggle Without a Limit

On the day of Pearl Harbor, Donald Nelson had an early lunch with a group that included a Supreme Court justice and the senator who was chairman of the Senate Foreign Relations Committee. As did so many conversations in those days, the talk turned to whether the United States would enter the war; the consensus was "not in the foreseeable future," Nelson recalled in *Arsenal of Democracy*.

The fact that otherwise knowledgeable and influential Washington people could hold this opinion on the eve of the outbreak of global war was a good indicator of the enormity of the task facing American industry. As many Americans weren't prepared mentally or emotionally, neither was industry prepared physically for the incredible demands to come. When posters urged, "Increase production!" and "Stay on the job!" they were serious.

The exact state of America's lack of preparedness is shocking, in retrospect. In 1939, the country's emergency defense budget called for $3.3 billion, which may sound like a lot until you learn that at the beginning of 1942, that figure would be $131 billion. In May 1940, President Roosevelt asked for production of 50,000 warplanes and Congress authorized less than a hundred after bitter debate. American industry was producing 200 civilian planes per month.

The transformation of American industry was triggered during the five weeks immediately after Pearl Harbor, when the Allies were hemmed in on all fronts, subs were rumored to be prowling both coasts, the Pacific Fleet had been flattened and crucial raw materials were already being cut off by Japan from the South Pacific.

The needs of America's allies, especially the British, helped get the gears turning; England had declared war on Germany in September 1939, closely followed by France, Australia, New Zealand and Canada. The British placed orders for 26,000 planes with American industry. The importance of their defense and the comparative nearness of the Allies' potential enemies were dramatized in a poster by Max Gordon. It shows a pair of huge black boots, with a swastika on the sole, that are striding across the Atlantic Ocean from a burning England and are about to descend on the Statue of Liberty. "Help Britain Defend America—Speed Production," the caption says. The poster was produced by the Committee to Defend America by Aiding the Allies.

According to numerous historians, big business was reluctant to convert to war industries, even after

Next page
An entire genre of wartime posters identified the home front worker as a sort of soldier, sharing some of the challenges and urgency of actual combat. After national labor unions agreed to no-strike rules during wartime, absenteeism actually increased. In the months following Pearl Harbor, absenteeism rates rose 300 percent; causes included poor transportation, housing shortages and a lack of child care, as well as higher salaries that allowed people to afford to take time off. Nevertheless, wildcat strikes, sickness and absenteeism never amounted to more than one percent of all the time worked during the war. As one historian concluded, "The fruits of the remaining 99 percent had sealed the Axis' fate." During the war, not taking a day off was seen as a patriotic action. Ronald McLeod created this poster in 1944.

Previous page
The injured or wounded soldier was a rare element in posters early in the war but became increasingly common toward the end of the conflict. This poster is noteworthy for its lack of any other captions or logos.

Page 53
Victor Keppler's jolly Army Air Forces aviator in shearling flight gear dates from 1943. This poster looks like a wartime version of a baseball trading card.

"Keep pitching— we need those planes"

U. S. ARMY — AIR FORCES

Early in the war, President Franklin Roosevelt carefully introduced new habits and attitudes to American citizens. His plain-talking approach is evident in this excerpt, which deals with several related topics, including organized labor and product shortages. This excerpt is from Roosevelt's address to the nation on February 23, 1942.

In every part of the country, experts in production and the men and women at work in the plants are giving loyal service. With few exceptions, labor, capital, and farming realize that this is no time either to make undue profits or to gain special advantages, one over the other.

We are calling for new plants and additions to old plants and for plant conversion to war needs. We are seeking more men and more women to run them. We are working longer hours. We are coming to realize that one extra plane or extra tank or extra gun or extra ship completed tomorrow may, in a few months, turn the tide on some distant battlefield; it may make the difference between life and death for some of our fighting men. We know now that if we lose this war it will be generations or even centuries before our conception of democracy can live again.

And we can lose this war only if we slow up our effort or if we waste our ammunition sniping at each other.

Here are three high purposes for every American:

1. We shall not stop work for a single day. If any dispute arises we shall keep on working while the dispute is solved by mediation, conciliation, or arbitration—until the war is won.

2. We shall not demand special gains or special privileges or advantages for any one group or occupation.

3. We shall give up conveniences and modify the routine of our lives if our country asks us to do so. We will do it cheerfully, remembering that the common enemy seeks to destroy every home and every freedom in every part of our land.

This generation of Americans has come to realize, with a present and personal realization, that there is something larger and more important than the life of any individual or of any individual group—something for which a man will sacrifice, and gladly sacrifice, not only his pleasures, not only his goods, not only his associations with those he loves, but his life itself. In time of crisis when the future is in the balance we come to understand, with full recognition and devotion, what this nation is, and what we owe it.

Pearl Harbor. Businesses and industries had valid reasons for hesitating. They doubted that big enough markets would exist after the war and felt that jobs would be scarce after the war. Furthermore, what would happen if they tackled immense expansion and then the war ended unexpectedly?

The wheels were slow to get turning. Federal plans had been for a $100 billion defense effort in 1941, but less than $20 billion was contracted for by that fall, and only $7 billion was spent by the end of the year. The news wasn't all dismal; the percentage of the United States' productivity going into defense tripled. On July 1, 1940, America was spending $165 million per month on defense. That figure reached $500 million per month on January 1, 1941, and $900 million per month the following July.

The statistics continued to jump, all pointing to what a British general would underline when he analyzed the war: "[The] battles were as much a tussle

Next page
Workers needed to feel that their labor was contributing to combat victories, as this poster suggests. Such battle scenes provided a vivid contrast to the factories and assembly lines back home. Herbert Morton Stoops created this poster in 1942 for the Army Ordnance Department. Stoops, an artillery officer during World War I, was one of the most prolific American illustrators of military scenes. He worked primarily in black-and-white, and was recognized as an expert on military and naval uniforms. During his career, he illustrated for newspapers in California and Chicago, did Western scenes for Bluebook *magazine, and contributed illustrations to* Collier's *and* Cosmopolitan.

Previous page
An easily recognizable symbol is a poster's stock in trade, and this poster contains two symbols that would become even more famous as the war progressed—the leather jacket and aircraft nose art. John Falter made this poster in 1942. It is credited "War Production Board—A7." Falter was just thirty-one when the war started, although he had already done illustrations for commercial magazines. He served in the Navy during the war as a special artist, producing some 180 posters, and later continued his career by illustrating books and magazines, including Reader's Digest.

Page 57
Although thousands of miles lay between domestic time clocks and combat beachheads, posters made the connection early and often. Amos Sewell created this one in 1943 for the Army Ordnance Department, a prolific producer of posters during the war. Sewell began doing magazine illustrations in 1936 and contributed to the Saturday Evening Post *for more than twenty years, reaching a height of popularity in the forties and fifties.*

READY FOR ANYTHING
thanks to you!

next of kin has been notified...

YOUR WORK WILL SAVE LIVES

The gray flesh tones and funereal lighting add to the somber mood of this poster, which combines seriousness and sentimentality.

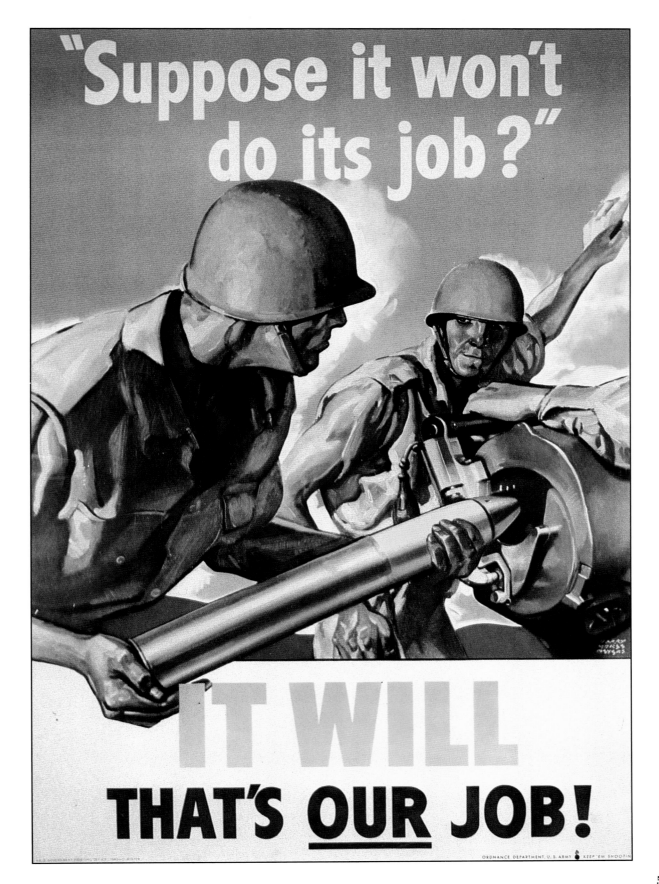

Previous page
The use of war-related products in combat offered quality assurance personnel a golden opportunity for stressing the importance of maintaining quality standards while production was skyrocketing and manufacturers were facing stricter and stricter deadlines. Harry Morse Meyers made this poster for the Army Ordnance Department in 1942.

between competing factories as between contending armies. . . . God now marched with the biggest industries rather than with the biggest battalions," he said.

President Roosevelt pushed early and hard for speed and expansion. According to one account, his habitual way of signing important memoranda was to write, "Work fast—FDR."

A 1942 poster from the Sheldon-Claire Company of Chicago sounded the same urgent note. It said,

Not all wartime posters were created by professional artists. This amateur poster was created by David White and Walter Soroka for the Joint War Production Drive Committee, Vought-Sikorsky Aircraft, in 1942. Early in the war, Vought-Sikorsky was a division of United Aircraft Corporation, which was in turn a large American manufacturer of airframes, aircraft engines and propellors.

"Every job is a fighting man's job. Minutes count with freedom at stake. Let's cram them full of work! Produce for victory!" Why the hurry? Because a four-engine bomber took 90,000 working hours to build.

To the WPB fell the thorny task of meshing the civilian economy—most facets of which had to be maintained—and the exploding demands of the military. It was by no means smooth sailing. The WPB frequently squabbled with the Army over who would control war production and over the importance of the civilian economy. After Pearl Harbor, Donald Nelson recalled, the military "adopted what was to be their policy for the duration: astronomical quantities of everything and to hell with civilian needs."

In Nelson's view, the military often wanted to dictate to civilian industry how it should accomplish its task. Nelson opposed this notion, feeling that government planners should leave industry alone to execute the orders. For Nelson, the issue took on philosophical overtones: "Merely to inflict military defeat on our enemies was not enough," he wrote. "We had to do it our own way." Nelson believed America had to prove that democracy was "more efficient, more productive, more able to respond to the demands of a great emergency than the dictatorial system of our enemies."

Aircraft makers, like those who designed and built all the other crucial weapons, shared the knowledge that if they didn't meet the need of their new "customers"—the soldiers, marines and sailors—they wouldn't just lose business, they would be letting down the war effort, causing unnecessary problems or pain for the people at the front, perhaps even endangering their lives. This perception was drummed into civilian workers through numerous posters and in fact became a central theme of the on-the-job genre.

Work was never in short supply; more often, workers were. In the case of aircraft factories, the hunt for workers was, in Nelson's words, "a masterpiece of promotion and evangelism." Retirees came back to work, and employees took on night jobs. The factories sent out trucks equipped with loudspeakers to announce openings, hired bands to appear at free shows, opened special offices in towns and even sent agents door to door to hire people. The WPB even found jobs for the 200,000 prisoners in the federal prisons. At San Quentin, convicts made camouflage strips and sirens.

Civilian employment in industry skyrocketed. The civilian economy expanded from 48 million workers in 1940 to 54 million in 1944, in addition to the 12 million men who had joined the service. The growth was

Next page
Usually, if a product didn't work, the manufacturer simply faced a disgruntled customer and perhaps a nasty letter. During the war, all that changed. This 1942 poster involves the viewer in a small combat drama that illustrates the point. The artist was John Vickery, working for the Army Ordnance Department.

"God help me if this is a dud!"

HIS LIFE IS IN YOUR HANDS

61

apparent in every sector of industry. In 1939, the aircraft industry had a work force of 48,000. By November 1943, it had grown to more than 2 million, including almost 500,000 women.

This rapid growth triggered a number of problems: housing, labor relations and the unusually close proximity of male and female workers. On a day-to-day basis, however, a plant supervisor's major concerns were to get all the workers to show up and once they did, to keep them from getting hurt. Pressures to speed production, installation of new machines and assembly lines, inexperienced workers and short training schedules all combined to make the wartime work place a virtual battle zone. Safety campaigns took on added importance, and absenteeism was no longer a matter of laziness or of wanting to take an afternoon off to go to a ball game—it was a matter of patriotism. And if getting a job, showing up every day, working plenty of overtime and keeping safe weren't enough, workers were importuned at every opportunity to buy war bonds, as well.

From early in the war, civilian workers were portrayed as soldiers on the home front and asked to think of themselves as equally important and equally crucial to victory when compared with military soldiers. In 1941, Cyrus Hungerford produced a poster with the slogan, "You are a production soldier . . . America's First Line of Defense is Here." Hungerford used this slogan on a series of posters dealing with a range of topics including security and rumor control.

The day shift—lunch boxes in hand, hard hats on head—lines up in front of the time clocks at the Bethlehem-Fairfield shipyards in Baltimore, Maryland. The billboard overhead offers a familiar wartime message. Scenes such as this one make it hard to believe that workers were in short supply. Arthur Siegel made this photo for the Office of War Information in May 1943. Library of Congress.

Service people died during the war: the death toll was 292,000 American soldiers, with another 671,000 wounded. But did soldiers and sailors suffer greater hazards, pains and hardships than civilians? The military death rate was five in 1,000. On the home front, the death rate was more than twice that high, and the rates of death and injury in the war industries were higher still. In one plant that had 10,000 workers, 200 injuries per day was the norm. During the war, nearly 300,000 workers were killed, more than 1 million were disabled and 3 million were injured. These facts underline the message of this poster, done by Harry Morse Meyers in 1943 for the War Department Safety Council.

In a poster by Jean Carlu titled "Give 'em both barrels," the silhouettes of a machine gunner and a riveter are matched. The pattern for this type of poster was set back in the First World War. For example, a poster by Roy Hull Still for the Army Ordnance

Prize-Winning Poster Suggested By
HAMILTON MAY - DEPT. 5 - H.S.P. - WESTERLY

The artwork is fairly crude, but the message is unmistakable. In ordinary life, people who skipped work were simply lazy. During wartime, the ante was raised considerably. Hamilton May created this poster for the Joint War Production Drive Committee of Hamilton Standard Propellors, a division of United Aircraft Corporation.

Department showed a civilian worker in the background, at work on a machine gun; in the foreground was a trio of soldiers in a foxhole, firing the same gun. The text said, "Team work wins! Your work here makes their work over there possible. With your help they are invincible. Without it they are helpless. Whatever you make, machine gun or harness, cartridges or helmet, they are waiting for it."

If Nelson felt that the WPB's goal was to prove that democracy was more responsive and productive than fascism, the proof was not long in arriving. Looking back at the record, the only risk is statistical overdose. Once planning and construction turned the corner, America's shipyards and airplane factories were the greatest in the world. They were soon producing 10,000 aircraft per month and a 14,000 ton Liberty ship in a matter of weeks.

FDR's plan for 1942 included 45,000 tanks and 20,000 guns. A War Production Board poster in 1942 shows FDR at the apex of a huge V-shape, out of which is rising a dense stream of aircraft. Its caption says, "In 1942 America will build 60,000 war planes . . . In 1943 America will build 125,000 war planes." The 1943 plan also called for 75,000 tanks and 35,000 antiaircraft guns. The figures seemed inconceivable. And the final tally surpassed them. Between the time France fell and V-J Day, American industry produced 300,000 planes; 41 billion rounds of ammo; 100,000 tanks and armored cars; 2.4 million military trucks; 15 million rifles, pistols and machine guns; 64,000 landing craft; 5,400 merchant ships; and 6,500 Navy ships. The final bill for industrial production was $186 billion.

Small wonder, wrote Allan Nevins in his 1946 essay *How We Felt about the War,* that "people found a growing exhilaration . . . in the vast productive feats of America's rapidly mobilized war industries."

Yet you run the risk of misunderstanding the war effort if you think of it simply in terms of machines and technology. In 1941, poet Archibald MacLeish wrote in the foreword to *The American Cause,* "A free people cannot fight fascism unless it believes with even greater conviction that freedom is good and can be attained and that slavery is evil and can be opposed; that unless we regain in this democracy the conviction that there are final things for which democracy will fight—unless we recover a faith in the expression of these things in words—we can leave our planes unbuilt and our battleships on paper, for we shall not need them."

WPB director Donald Nelson earned a share of the war's verdict. Production, he wrote, was "a final test of what our democracy could do. It was the ultimate showdown. . . . It was as clear as anything can be that our enemies were betting their national existence on the belief that our democracy could not meet the test. And the test was met on a thousand different occasions." It was, he added, "probably the greatest collective achievement of all time. It [made] the 'seven wonders' of the ancient world look like the doodlings of a small boy on a rainy Saturday afternoon."

Emil Linn (left) sells Alva McWilliams the first "buy a bomber" bond at an Oldsmobile plant. McWilliams is credited with thinking up the "buy a bomber" drive, although such drives seem to have been common during the war. Oldsmobile History Center.

Jean Carlu created this poster for the Office for Emergency Management's Division of Information in 1942 or 1943. Carlu was born in France and had emerged a leading French graphic designer by the mid twenties. He produced numerous advertisements, adopting a succession of modernist techniques including cubist and surrealist approaches. In the thirties, he founded the Office de Propagande de la Paix, producing a number of disarmament posters. Carlu went to New York in 1940 to organize part of the French pavilion at the world's fair and remained in that city after the fall of France, designing and producing posters for the American war effort. He also served as an advisor to OWI, producing this poster. Although this poster is both well-known and successful, it drew wartime criticism because some people thought the worker's cap made him look like a gangster.

Air raid wardens meet in Zone 9, Southwest Area, Washington, DC. Posters, such as the famous one by Carlu at right, helped brighten the typically makeshift headquarters. Gordon R. Parks made this photo for the Office of War Information in July 1942. Library of Congress.

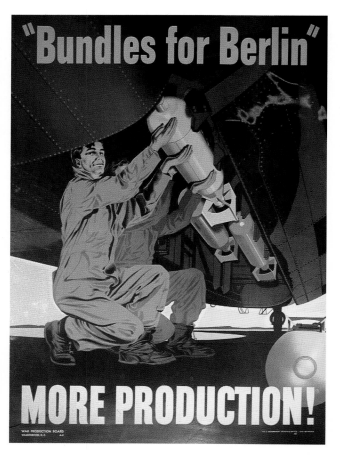

Simple alliteration and a sense of humor make this poster effective. The slogan is a takeoff on Bundles for Britain, an American relief effort for victims of the London blitz. In that case, the bundles were clothes. In this poster, as always, the portrayal of home front workers put them as close to combat as possible.

Next page
Military personnel gave numerous messages by means of posters to the folks at home. At one extreme were accusations and guilt-producing messages. At the other were cheerful expressions of gratitude, such as this one by Howard Scott, produced in 1943 for the Industrial Incentive Division, US Navy. Scott was a New Yorker and a member of the Society of Illustrators.

OFFICIAL U.S. TREASURY POSTER

This poster aimed at making purchases of war bonds and stamps more tangible. It was issued to enlist the help of schools to buy parts for jeeps. It shows the various parts of a jeep and the cost of each. When a school contributed the $1,165 to buy all nineteen major parts, the Treasury Department issued a citation to the school. Part of the poster text contains instructions about the program. Aircraft manufacturers ran similar campaigns with the theme of "buy a bomber" aimed at employees.

Previous page
When car manufacturers stopped making automobiles, some started to make a close relative—the tank, shown in the background of this poster. The artist was named Hewitt, possibly Donald Hewitt. He created this garishly lit poster for the War Finance Division of the Treasury Department in 1943.

Chapter 4

Women, Minorities and Children in the War

"We Can't Win Without Them"

Away from the world of politics and fame, on a personal and family level, the effects of military mobilization are easy to picture. Americans gave up their sons and husbands to an unknown future, with no guarantee they'd ever see them again. One result was an increasingly serious shortage of what they called in those prefeminism days *manpower*. The term was accurate at the beginning of the war, but its correctness soon became questionable.

Managers in many industries faced twin problems: workers were scarce and key employees had been drafted. The United States called for soldiers and sailors to aim weapons at the enemy, but it also needed workers to stay home and help make those weapons. Workers in some industries were exempt from the draft, and others scrambled to see if they were, too. The Office of War Information (OWI) files in the National Archives contain a letter from a member of the Graphic Arts Victory Committee in New York to Ralph Shikes of the OWI in February 1943 that deals with the problem:

Could you by any chance get some ruling on the essentiality of the printing industry, its business and its workmen? Newspapers are rated high on the essential list . . . would that make the printing ink maker essential, too; the plate-maker, the manufacturer of rollers? The Committee is being asked these questions, and it would be grand to have an answer.

To draw in the people who were unemployed and not eligible for military service, federal and civilian

Madelon O'Leary, a punch press operator in the Marine Division of Bendix Aviation Corporation, typifies the wartime's Rosie the Riveter. Even wearing coveralls, she no doubt drew her share of wolf whistles from male workers unaccustomed to women in the work place. James Abbe, Jr., made this photo for the Office of War Information in 1943. Library of Congress.

Previous page
Women at work in heavy industry were unusual figures before the war but quickly became familiar images. Courtney Allen created this Official U.S. Treasury Poster in 1944. Note the logo of the Sixth War Loan, which shows a bomb striking a rising-sun flag.

Previous page
This poster gives a candid view of the reasons for enlisting women in the military. Although the poster says "Distributed by OWI for the U.S. Marine Corps," the unusual credit line for a civilian firm—"McCandlish Litho. Corp., Philadelphia, PA"—suggests that the McCandlish company designed or produced the poster itself, or did both. The poster is undated, in contrast to the posters produced by the Government Printing Office, which were scrupulously dated and numbered.

The men on recruiting posters were always handsome, and the women were always pretty. In either case, they provided attractive role models for potential enlistees. In this case, a poster decorates local efforts to drum up interest in the Navy's WAVES. This photo is from the scrapbook of Ensign Lula Windham, who served as a WAVES recruiter during the war in Connecticut and New Jersey. War Memorial Museum of Virginia.

recruiters organized vast employment campaigns. In addition to the people who were previously unemployed and the men who weren't drafted because of their health or age, the drives targeted retirees and workers who could moonlight. During 1941, nearly 5.5 million workers were placed in defense industries. In the course of the war, the American work force increased from 45 million to more than 65 million.

Women made up a hefty percentage of the increased work force. About one quarter of all women were doing volunteer work in officially approved war programs, but this was only a small part of the work that had to be done. Three million women went to work who wouldn't otherwise have started punching a time clock at the factory.

In 1940, some 12 million women were employed nationwide. By 1944, that number had risen to 18.2 million. A total of 3.5 million women were at work with 6 million men on armament assembly lines in 1944. In the steel, machinery, shipbuilding, aircraft and auto industries, 1.7 million women were employed in 1944, compared with 233,000 five years earlier.

Civilian recruiters specifically targeted women with a number of campaigns, ultimately creating a classic and memorable caricature of the war, Rosie the Riveter, celebrated in both drawing and song. In *Since You Went Away*, Donald Rogers recalled her as a "long-lashed, snub-nosed, rosy-mouthed, buxom lass wearing coveralls and with a blue bandanna on her head." She was a far cry from the nearly nude pinup girls who were the mainstay of GI barracks, but Rosie was a heroine in her own way. Her presence on the production lines was no luxury. It was mandatory.

Rosie wasn't solely a Yank phenomenon, either— she had a British counterpart. A poster by Adolph Treidler is titled "My girls a WOW [woman ordnance worker]." It shows a grinning, helmeted soldier holding a photo of his girlfriend, who is wearing a badge and has a bandana around her head.

According to D'Ann Campbell, "Government manpower experts concerned with staffing the war factories realized their uphill battle: 'Women must be induced to change their customary life pattern of school, a few years of work, marriage and children. Some must remain in jobs, others must go to work.' Hence a vast propaganda campaign directed by the government in cooperation with all the media tried to induce women to change their life-cycle preferences."

Once they put on coveralls and started punching a time clock, women performed well. Foremen discovered that the main difference between men and women was the amount of weight they could carry, a problem that could be overcome by redesigning tasks and using machinery to lift and move heavy materials. In some plants, women outproduced men when they were doing identical tasks, particularly those calling for manual dexterity. Engineering studies determined that women did better than men at jobs requiring sharp eyes, flexible wrists, and delicate touch. Women handled repetitive motion better than men, and were more exact. Not exactly descriptions of riveting, but one of valuable skills for innumerable industrial tasks.

Early in the war, in many places, women were a novelty and subject to wolf whistles and leers. Campbell describes an aircraft factory in Detroit where managers had to relocate female workers because the men were wasting so much time "whistling and ogling." The workers faced enough safety hazards already, no doubt.

Women were welcome to go to work, but promotions were hard to come by in the predominantly male world of industry. The 1940 census listed 410,000 men as managers and officials in manufacturing, and only 18,000 women. Women were only temporarily wel-

Next page
Combat produced more than victories and dramatic battle scenes. This appeal to nurses accentuates one other inescapable result: wounded and disabled veterans.

73

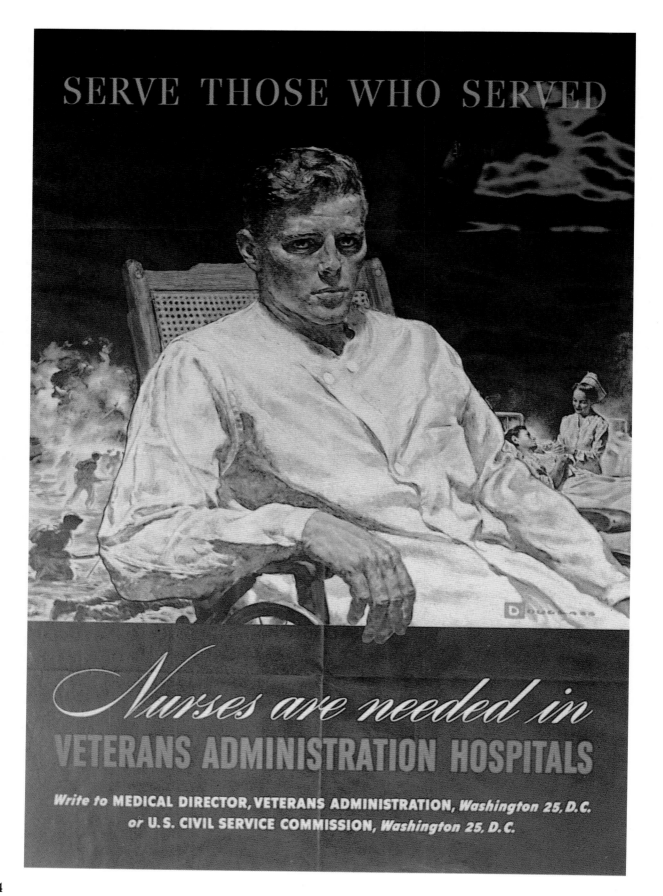

come in labor unions, or not welcome at all. In 1940, the "hostile" unions—mainly construction, railroads and mining—had about four percent of their membership made up of women. That percentage had tripled by 1943, and during the war, most unions accepted female members. However, after the war, they quickly got rid of them. Between 1944 and 1946, unions shed forty-three percent of their women members, and in 1946 only six percent were left. The union's attitudes and actions were not just arbitrary malevolence; they were in fact understandable. "No one who switched into and out of the labor force, and who proclaimed primary loyalty to the family, could fit the intensely masculine image of the brotherhood banded together," Campbell wrote in *Women at War with America*.

War posters painted a stirring, classical portrait of the man as soldier. Those same posters took snapshots of a greater variety of aspects of the wartime experience of women. On one hand is the image of Rosie the Riveter, helping produce the tools of war. In 1942, the War Manpower Commission produced a poster that said, "Women in the war—we can't win without them." It showed a woman working on a bomb with a power tool. On the other hand are the images of wives and mothers, the roles that most of the Rosies were anxious to get back to, and that symbolized the "home" that soldiers were fighting the war to defend.

Although government officials were anxious to get women to work in industrial jobs and elsewhere, they worried about possible negative effects. In the summer of 1942, the Office of War Information's Special Services Division studied the war's effects on the family. It found many pros and cons. The increased absence of women from the home was a negative, since it could affect child care. Also, women's growing financial independence was leading to an increased emotional independence that the OWI found might weaken marriages. Many wives found that they enjoyed their job—they got a chance to learn new skills and become more self-confident, less dependent. Many husbands, in fact, began to worry that their wives wouldn't want to stop working after the war. By and large, these fears were answered—and put to rest—by the baby boom. Most women were anxious to hang up the tool belt and put on the apron once again.

Just as women entered the civilian work force, some also entered the military. "Making women soldiers was the most dramatic break with traditional sex roles that occurred in the twentieth century," Campbell wrote. Although the drama was only hinted at in most posters, it provides an important subtext to what the posters showed. Since women never accounted for more than two percent of the total military population, more illustrations might have been misleading.

Women could do numerous jobs in the military. A World War I poster from England announces, "British Women!—the Royal Air Force needs your help as clerks, waitresses, cooks, experienced motor cyclists, and in many other capacities . . ." Female volunteers served in Britain and the United States during World War I. More than 11,000 served as nurses and as what the Navy called yeoman (F), the Navy term for clerks, secretaries and office workers. As a rule, in both wars, women usually served in jobs that were identical to what they had done as civilians.

The military needed battalions of clerks and office workers. If women could fill those jobs, that meant the men could move to the battlefronts. A British poster, for example, says, "Join the Wrens [Women's Royal Navy Service] and free a man to join the fleet." American posters sounded the same theme.

By Pearl Harbor, England and Canada were recruiting women. In March 1942, Congress passed the Women's Auxiliary Army Corps (WAAC) Act, which gave women partial military status. The WAAC became the Women's Army Corps (WAC) in June 1943.

In July 1942, women who wanted to enlist began to be accepted into the Navy as full-fledged reservists. They were known as Women Accepted for Volunteer Emergency Service (WAVES). The Coast Guard followed by creating the Spars (from the Coast Guard motto, *Semper Paratus*) in November 1942, and in February 1943, the Marines also began accepting women.

At peak strength, 271,000 women served in the armed forces: 100,000 WACs, 86,000 WAVES, 17,600 Marines, 10,000 Spars, 47,000 Army Nurse Corps members and 11,000 Navy Nurse Corps members. Some of the women in the last two categories were from the Cadet Nurse Corps, a federal training program that sent 125,000 nurses through school between 1943 and 1948. Slightly more than one thousand served as Women's Air Service Pilots, although they weren't recognized as members of the military service.

The recruiting posters aimed at women are good examples of how misleading posters can be. Behind the scenes was a huge amount of reluctance toward the idea of women as soldiers. The Navy, Marines and Coast Guard had relatively small quotas and managed to fill them. The Army, however, had a hard time, even though "Madison Avenue advertising agencies helped coordinate intensive nationwide media campaigns [and] censorship prevented unflattering stories or photographs from appearing," as Campbell wrote.

A 1943 Gallup poll found five reasons for a shortage of women volunteers: women didn't care about the war, they were afraid of Army life and regimentation, they didn't understand the jobs the WAAC did, their relatives or husbands opposed their volunteering and they felt that the Army itself was hostile to women. That fourth reason was still around two years later, when an

Next page
Despite widespread opposition to women in the armed services, few questioned that women made the best nurses. An artist named Bernatchke created this poster in 1945. The poster offers many options for action, indicating the unusual cooperation that existed during the war: The motivated viewer could write to the Surgeon General, visit an Army recruiting station or go to a Red Cross office.

636

NURSES ARE NEEDED NOW!

IF YOU ARE A REGISTERED NURSE AND NOT YET 45 YEARS OF AGE
APPLY TO THE SURGEON GENERAL, UNITED STATES ARMY,
WASHINGTON 25, D. C., OR TO ANY RED CROSS PROCUREMENT OFFICE

ARMY NURSE CORPS

INFORMATIONAL PAMPHLETS MAY BE OBTAINED AT U. S. ARMY RECRUITING STATIONS

Army survey in June 1945 revealed that sixty-four percent of the soldiers surveyed would not advise their girlfriend to join the WAC and twenty percent probably would not.

The attitude that military work wasn't feminine or was too dangerous or demeaning fostered the competing views of women in wartime that show up on posters. Although men tend to be portrayed as either workers or soldiers, women reveal several additional roles. They appear as inactive patriots who bravely give up their men. Sometimes they are shown as frugal housewives, doing their share by saving gas and salvaging tin cans. And sometimes they are shown as damsels in distress. As far back as 1918, a poster was captioned "This may be *Your* Sister's Fate." It shows Germans dragging away a frightened young woman. Its theme was still useful and effective during the Second World War.

Although the nostalgic tendency is to recall the war years as a time of wonderful unanimity and national solidarity, the home front experience had downsides, as well. It is only by recognizing them that you appreciate what posters and similar messages were trying to accomplish and why the task wasn't easy.

Paychecks were great, but the social effects of the employment boom weren't all positive. Millions of workers were shoved around the United States in search of jobs or drawn by the lure of higher wages. Countless families, perhaps already minus a husband or sons, were uprooted from small hometowns and plunged into teeming industrial centers that were woefully short of housing.

At least 4 million women were wives of servicemen, and most of those servicemen were draftees who were drawing paychecks that were much smaller than the average civilian wage. Although many women did go to work outside the home, many others didn't. For those who didn't, the result was a standard of living reminiscent of the Depression.

Clearly, Americans were inconvenienced, but things could have been much worse. Compare the problems in American society with those in England. In all cases, America's problems seemed, if not trivial, at least modest. Although tens of thousands of American families were displaced, the effects—as was the case with rationing—were far worse across the Atlantic.

In America, some fathers were in the service and growing numbers of mothers were working at jobs as well as at home, but still the families were essentially united. In England, however, 1.5 million schoolchildren and mothers with children unther the age of five were evacuated from potential bombing targets. Unlike the flood of false alarms about air raids that hit the West Coast of the United States after Pearl Harbor, the threat in England was real. London was bombed for more than ten weeks in a row beginning in September 1940. During the next year, more British civilians were killed than soldiers.

These comparisons worked their way into a 1941 poster by Cyrus Hungerford, one of his series that car-

ried the slogan "You are a production soldier." This poster said, "Thanksgiving—No blitzkrieg! No bomb proof shelters! No concentration or slave labor camps! Let's keep it that way!" The ways that workers could accomplish that goal were only implied on this particular poster but were to become increasingly well-known thanks to a spate of similar posters: work harder, don't take time off, avoid accidents, and figure out ways to do a job faster and cheaper.

In *While You Were Gone,* Margaret Mead summed up the domestic side of the home front as "a thousand little irritations and no big ones." Americans weren't starved or bombed out. They were safe from witnessing the horrors of the battlefronts. And both men and women could do plenty of things to keep busy and to contribute to the effort.

Discrimination was more than a little irritation, however, and it permeated American life during the war. When the Red Cross staged massive blood drives, it announced that blood from black donors would be separated out. United Service Organizations (USO) clubs were segregated. At the beginning of the war, the Navy would accept blacks only as cooks and stewards, changing this rule in April 1942. The Marines wouldn't accept them at all until June 1942. The Army drafted black soldiers but made many of them pick-and-shovel specialists or stevedores.

Racial prejudice was well recognized during the war; it isn't a problem that was perceived only in retrospect. Arthur Upham Pope was chairman of the Committee for National Morale. Writing in a 1942 book called *America Organizes to Win the War,* he pointed out, "We say glibly that in the United States of America all men are free and equal, but do we treat them as if they were? Far from it. There is religious and racial prejudice everywhere in the land, and if there is a greater obstacle anywhere to the attainment of the teamwork we must have, no one knows what it is." He continued, "We expect the Negroes to serve in our fighting forces—and we see to it that they do serve—but we don't expect them to serve as equals. The less said about our treatment of them as citizens, the better."

Small wonder that blacks and other minorities are strikingly absent from posters. Joe Louis appeared on one poster, but he was already famous when the war started, and black celebrities hardly seem to count as authentic representatives of minorities. Later in the war, the government worked to recognize the contributions of average minority folks, too. For example, in 1943, the War Production Board released a poster that

Next page
OWI poster number 28 appeared in 1943 and depicted women in another role, as home front consumer. When the war started, the United States was importing more than ninety percent of its rubber from the Far East. When Japan seized control of that region, rationing was inevitable. Tire and gas rationing also meant that many stores stopped delivering groceries and other items. The artist's name was Sarra.

showed "ex-private Obie Bartlett," a black soldier who had lost an arm at Pearl Harbor and was working as a welder in a shipyard. Bartlett is quoted on the poster: "Somtimes I feel my job here is as important as the one I had to leave," he says. The poster does two jobs at once: it also builds worker morale.

Compared to women and minorities, children played the smallest role in wartime posters. Even though they appeared as props in posters, the war altered their lives, too.

Children missed their fathers who were off fighting and their mothers who went to work during the days. They found plenty to do.

"The old game of cops and robbers turned into Marines and Japs," one observer noted. But kids were involved in more than mere play.

School kids pulled wagons from house to house, collecting paper and tin cans. They cut the ends of the cans out, smashed the cans flat and turned them in at the neighborhood fire station, an officially designated collection site.

Boy Scouts collected more than 3 million books, 109 million pounds of rubber and 23 million pounds of tin. Scouts also distributed more than a million posters per month for the Office of War Information, and distributed millions of price control pamphlets and consumer pledges as well. Not that the Scouts were always on the job, as this letter shows:

January 19, 1944

Mr. Howard R. Patton
Boy Scouts of America
2 Park Avenue
New York 16, New York

Dear Howard:

While in New York on Monday I rode on an open Fifth Avenue bus from thirty-fourth to fifty-seventh street and return . . . virtually the entire commercial length of the avenue, and was both surprised and disappointed to find NOT ONE SINGLE POSTER as a result of last Saturday's distribution.

I frankly have no idea what the reason for this is nor where the fault lies, (surely a lack of gasoline cannot be blamed here) but I do know that any distribution system that fails completely to achieve even a token showing on the nation's number one thoroughfare must have something very wrong with it.

I would appreciate having any ideas you may have as to how this deplorable situation may be corrected.

With kindest personal regards.

Jacques DunLany
Chief of the Division
Poster Clearance and Allocation
Room 3339, Social Security Building

Treasury Secretary Henry Morgenthau, Jr., who was notably successful at enlisting many well-known

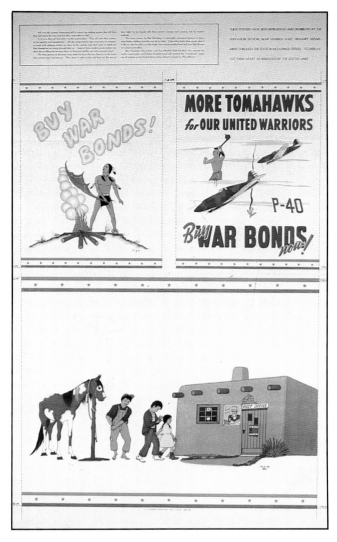

The junior artists who made this poster were Eva Mirabel, who signed it Eah-Ha-Wa; Charles Presbetonequa; and Ben Quintana, who signed it Ha-a-tee-Ben. It was issued by the Education Section of the Treasury Department's War Savings Staff (WSS). The three posters on the sheet were intended to be cut out and posted separately. The artists were students at the US Indian School in Santa Fe, New Mexico. The poster's text says, in part, "All over the country Americans still in school are making posters that tell how they feel about the war, and how they want others to feel. In a way, they all feel alike—as the posters show. They all want their country to win quickly and triumphantly. All the poster-makers urge us to save, to conserve, to work with whatever talents we have at the wartime jobs that come to hand. . . . Some of the student poster-makers say these things differently because they see America and the war with a special vision. The three posters on this page were made by [students] who see America as the home their people have always had. They share it with us now and they see the war as their fight—to be fought with their ancient courage and cunning, but by modern methods." The poster is dated 1942 and is listed as WSS poster number 625; if the Treasury Department had produced more than 600 posters by 1942, that figure serves as a gauge of the flood of posters to come.

79

"above and beyond the call of duty"

DORIE MILLER
Received the Navy Cross
at Pearl Harbor, May 27, 1942

Previous page

Previous page
Dorie Miller was an early hero of the war. He was stationed aboard USS West Virginia *at her berth in Pearl Harbor on December 7, 1941. The ship took hits by two heavy bombs and six torpedoes. Miller carried the dying skipper to safety, then returned to man a machine gun against dive-bombers that were still attacking the ship. Since he was a mess attendant, he hadn't been trained to use the gun, but he was a careful enough observer to operate it. Miller received the Navy Cross for his bravery in May 1942 and was later reported missing after the sinking of USS* Liscombe Bay. *David Stone Martin created this poster in 1943.*

artists for his war loan campaigns, didn't neglect youngsters when targeting sales drives. Schoolchildren, usually spending dimes and quarters, bought $2 billion worth of war stamps during the course of the war and sold more than $1 billion worth of stamps and bonds in various campaigns.

Kids faced their own shortages, too. Santa's elves made no electric or mechanical trains, ice skates, sleds, bicycles, BB guns, toy cars or wagons during the war. After the war, plenty of two-year-olds had never had a rubber ball. Plastics made up some of the difference. Kids may have been pleased to find that when they left their plastic trucks out in the rain, they didn't rust, as the metal versions had.

The Treasury Department's campaigns to sell war bonds and stamps targeted both adults and children, as evidenced by this 1945 poster, and children responded by buying millions of dollars worth. The well-known Disney signature is at lower left. The poster credit line says "D'Arcy Printing and Litho. Corp., NY 1-31-45."

Chapter 5

Propaganda, Art or Advertising?

Stirring Volatile Emotions

War-era posters can now cost thousands of dollars. People put them in expensive frames and hang them on their living-room walls. Do these actions mean that the posters are art? The word *art* conjures up positive images of unusual beauty, intense perception and deep meaning, but the word has many other definitions. In one sense, it simply means a specific skill, craft or profession—*Webster's New World Dictionary* lists "the cobbler's art" as an example. The word can mean fine arts, but it can also mean the illustrations in newspapers and magazines, as distinguished from the text. From *art* comes the word *artifice* (as *craftiness* comes from *craft*), implying deception and trickery.

Taken as a group, all these definitions apply to war posters through the years. The question of whether posters are propaganda, art or advertising cannot be answered with a single choice. The spectrum of critical opinion about posters is mirrored in the changing definition of the word *propaganda*. The word began with a positive meaning; it meant the spreading of religious faith. Next, it assumed a neutral, civilian meaning; according to *Webster's*, it meant "any systematic, widespread dissemination or promotion of particular ideas, doctrines, practices, etc. to further one's own cause or to damage an opposing one." Finally, it seems to have ended up with a negative meaning; *Webster's*

The Nazis issued this anti-American poster in France in 1943. To the Allies, this poster was propaganda of the nastiest, most misleading sort. To the Nazis—who knows? The perverse smirk on FDR's face may have seemed like a vicious but accurate editorial cartoon. As always, children were useful props. Naval Historical Center.

Previous page
The depictions of combat in war posters tend to be quite realistic, but the scene in this poster, created by Ferdinand Warren in 1942, is so busy and compressed that it looks like an advertisement for a movie, as opposed to a pitch for war bonds. The technique is relatively crude, and the scene is cluttered with ships, tanks, machine gunners and aircraft overhead. The lighting in particular looks as if it has been staged in a studio. Warren was from Independence, Missouri; his paintings were exhibited at the Metropolitan Museum of Art.

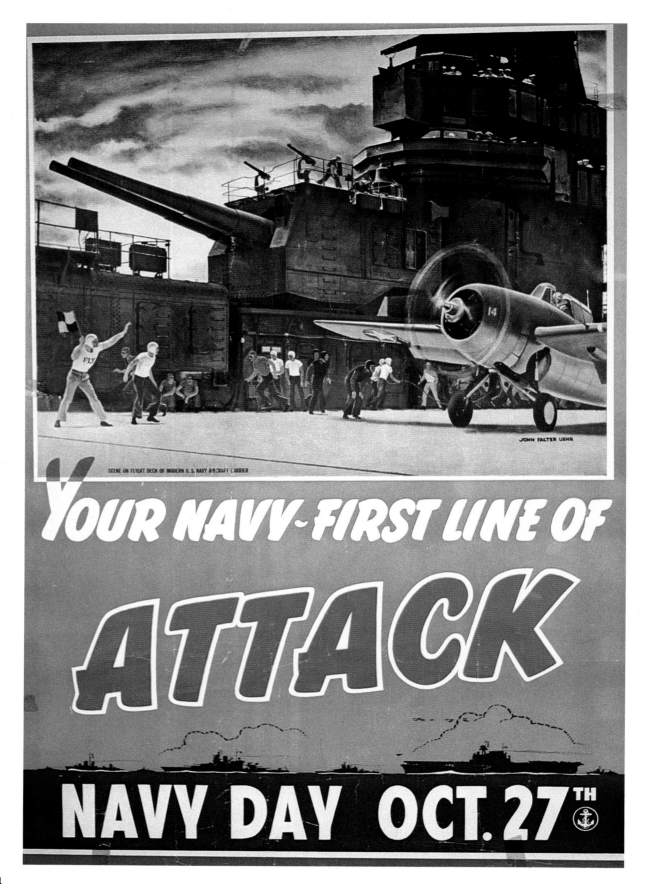

says it is "now often used disparagingly to connote deception or distortion."

Perhaps our feelings about a poster simply depend on our ideological perspective. If the poster agrees with our beliefs, it is valuable and true. If it disagrees, it is propaganda, a dangerous lie.

Although posters have had a long and useful life as a means of promoting commercial products, most people shy away from thinking of war posters as advertisements. Commercial ads seem trivial. War posters deal with life, death, truth, justice and the fate of nations. Actually, the relationship between posters and advertising isn't as distant as it might appear. In discussing the British posters of World War I, author Peter Stanley pointed out that the posters were usually designed by tradespeople, not artists, who were used to producing commercial ads. As a result, Stanley wrote, "the posters resembled pre-war advertisements." He cited an unsigned poster headlined "The kitchen is the [key] to victory," with a picture of a key substituted for the word *key*. Stanley said this poster "could almost have been advertising a type of kitchen range or a brand of gravy."

The producers of the early commercial posters were not interested in aesthetic debates; their bottom line was effectiveness. An article in the February 1914 issue of *The Poster* said, "The important thing about a poster is not its country or its date or the name of the artist, or its authenticity or any other fact about it—the important thing about it is its power to attract attention and sell goods."

Little by little, however, aesthetic concerns entered the debate. Early commentators on commercial posters didn't hesitate to use the word *art* and attached no stigma to the sales aspect. Writing in Amsterdam in 1929, Albert Hahn said, "What we are concerned with in art in advertising is a type of art seen by everybody, and one whose very nature enables it to influence even those people who care little for art and who, as a rule, would never consider entering an art gallery or an exhibition. It is street art pure and simple, and as such out and out popular."

Jean-Marie Moreau was a well-known poster artist who used the pseudonym A. M. Cassandre. He saw the poster as something primarily practical. In 1933, he wrote, "It is difficult to determine the status of the poster among the pictorial arts. Some reckon it as a department of painting, which is mistaken, others place it among the decorative arts and I believe they are no less mistaken.... Painting is an end in itself. The poster is only a means to an end, a means of communication between the dealer and the public, something like a telegraph. The poster designer plays a part of a telegraph official: he does not initiate news; he merely dispenses it." The clear-cut dispensing of information—civil defense procedures, rationing rules and the like—was certainly the job of a number of the less inspirational posters from World War II.

The notion of posters as a visual telegraph remained current and continued to serve as a gauge for the effectiveness of a poster. According to John Barnicoat, author of *A Concise History of Posters*, "By 1956, a writer on advertising from the United States, H. W. Hepner, could say that in designing a poster 'one should assume that the people who see it cannot or at least will not read it. It must tell its whole story in about six seconds.'" The most striking and effective of the World War II posters meet that criteria. The remaining question is, what was the story they were telling?

From the perspective of the people and the federal agencies who issued war posters—such as the Office of War Information, the military recruiters, the Treasury Department—the purpose of the poster was clear. It was "the weapon on the wall," in the phrase of writer Peter Stanley, author of *What Did You Do in the War, Daddy?* This wartime purpose was well established during World War I, when television and radio didn't exist, and the silent film industry was in its infancy. Posters had little competition as a means of inexpensive public communication. As Zbynek Zeman pointed out in *Selling the War*, "The modern forms of propaganda—leaflets dropped from aircraft, broadcasting (the most powerful propaganda weapon of the Second World War) and films—were not yet in existence, or were not used, in the first war."

To produce posters during World War I, the Committee on Public Information created a Division of Pictorial Publicity. That title sounds harmless, almost focused on public relations. Later instances of official terminology are equally interesting. If we produced *publicity* in World War I, the Office of War Information theoretically produced *information* in World War II. The British called a spade a spade when, before World War II started, they set up an agency called the Department of Propaganda to the Enemy and Enemy-Controlled Territories. They later changed the name to the Department for Enemy Propaganda.

Although all governments openly produced propaganda, the word *propaganda* quickly assumed sinister and destructive overtones, particularly when it was being produced by the enemy. A poster by Cyrus Hungerford dealt with that topic, with a subtheme of rumor control. Its text said, "Unpatriotic propaganda—beware gas attacks! Poison gas on the battlefront is paralyzing. So is propaganda gas on our Production Front. A vicious rumor is one of the Dictator's deadliest weapons. It starts with a whispering campaign and can do as much harm as an invading army—So beware of suspicious gossip. Put on a gas mask and walk right through!"

What were these rumors? It would take an entire book to recount them all, but Paul Fussell spends an interesting chapter on the topic in his book *Wartime*. In general, the goal was to convince the enemy soldiers and civilians that they were losing or were doomed and that their government was lying to them.

Three essays in the 1942 book *America Organizes to Win the War* reveal various facets of the contemporary attitude toward propaganda. One such essay was written by Henry Steele Commager, author and professor of American history at Columbia University. He wrote, "Democracy has faith in education and knows that the truth will make men free, Nazism perverts understanding and emotions through propaganda. Democracy exalts tolerance, Nazism exploits intolerance."

For Ladislas Farago, who was a consultant to the Committee for National Morale, the sources of enemy propaganda were villains. "The propagandists aren't after the work, but the workers," he wrote. "They are attempting not physical or mechanical sabotage, but mental and moral sabotage—something more subtle and much deadlier." Thus, we have posters like the rumor-control example mentioned above.

Finally, novelist Dorothy Fisher wrote, "In its bad meaning, propaganda is the presentation of facts so arranged as to make us believe that the whole of which each fact is a part is quite different from what really is. In everyday, plain language, propaganda, as it is often practiced, is lying."

If propaganda "perverts" emotions, what is the status of the American posters that were clearly aimed at stirring up the volatile emotions of the viewer, primarily fear and hatred of the enemy? A poster from the Office of War Information called this approach a war of ideas, and it produced a genre of poster radically different from the patriotic, the spiritual and the informational. "These posters, for example 'Stay on the job until every murdering Jap is wiped out!', were some of the most grotesque produced by the western Allies," Peter Stanley wrote.

The Army poster Stanley referred to is complex—it shows tired POWs marching in the background, while in the foreground a Japanese soldier clubs a bleeding GI. Inset is what looks like a clipping from a newspaper, headlined "5200 Yank Prisoners Killed by Jap Torture in Philippines; Cruel 'March of Death' described." In this poster, the viewer is given what seems to be solid information, implied by the newspaper. Yet posters are not sources of news, and certainly not sources of solid information, which was hard enough to come by in any format during the war, censorship being what it was. Confronted with a "March of Death" poster, objective viewers must ask themselves if they are being informed or manipulated.

Bataan figured into a later poster controversy, as Geoffrey Perrett pointed out in *Days of Sadness, Years of Triumph*: "Federal officials were suspected of manipulating the war news to boost bond sales," he wrote. "News of the Bataan Death March, for instance, was kept secret for nearly two years and then, without explanation, was released on the eve of the Fourth War Loan. For several days the sale of bonds doubled."

This genre of poster was not a dominant one during World War II. It had been mined more deeply during the First World War, and the public exhibited an increasingly negative reaction to that excessive propaganda. In fact, news of the Nazi atrocities was met with widespread skepticism; somewhat surprisingly, the Nazi death camps weren't exploited in American posters.

Most of what would be popularly categorized as propaganda was found on the leaflet, a popular weapon during World War II. Posters had to be used mainly in one's own country, but you could bombard the enemy on his or her home turf with leaflets. A cynical British joke during World War II said that the first

"Refugees trust German soldiers," this poster exclaims. The fall of France and its armed occupation by the German Army opened up fertile opportunities for what Americans would have derided as propaganda. This vision of the jovial Nazi would certainly not have appeared in an American poster.

bombs dropped by the British carried a label reading, "You are lucky; this might have been a leaflet."

Domestic posters contained enough exaggerated statements and questionable information to leave some historians critical of their intentions and techniques. Peter Stanley is at one extreme; he wrote, "Wartime posters campaigns were waged against civilian populations by their own governments."

Even O. W. Riegel, who was a propaganda analyst for the Office of War Information during World War II, is far from idealistic about the role of the poster. In a 1979 book about posters, he wrote, "The function of the war poster is to make coherent and acceptable a basically incoherent and irrational ordeal of killing, suffering, and destruction that violates every accepted principle of morality and decent living. This requires ingenuity and skill, as well as a predisposition of the audience to believe." As a result, he pointed out, "posters conceal the realities of the war behind a fog of propaganda," rarely showing someone being killed or maimed. The corpses in posters tend to be impersonal and vague.

To what extent complex, realistic truths can enter into posters is open to question. Posters are not a place for well-reasoned arguments or for discussions of strategy. By definition, a poster's message has to be simplistic and portrayed in familiar ideas and images; the viewer had to accept its message as conventional wisdom. If the distinction between right and wrong blurs, all bets are off.

Regardless of the propaganda content of war posters in general, their visual and emotional impact—then and now—is undeniable. Writing thirty years after the war, Zbynek Zeman said in *Selling the War*, "Many [posters] still succeed in evoking a particular period of the war, spelling out long-forgotten messages in a clear and direct language." Because the best posters were usually created by people working alone, the posters have "aged better than all other artifacts of propaganda," according to Zeman.

Critics and connoisseurs have long recognized why the "weapon on the wall" has such firepower. According to John Garrigan, the poster is "an immediate message and distillation of form and idea" that can "shock or entertain, stir the emotions, and linger in the memory. In this respect, the poster as a means of communication is still unsurpassed." If you have to stop to figure it out, a poster has already missed its chance.

"A poster can never be obscure," John Barnicoat wrote in *A Concise History of Posters*. "The designer cannot allow his work to express a private idea that subsequent generations may be able to unravel; he must achieve instant contact. To do this he must, like an entertainer, work with his audience."

O. W. Riegel agreed, writing that the poster must be "communicable even to the illiterate." The technique of an effective poster should be appreciated: "It is not only fast, it is extremely precise," he wrote.

Sergeant Ardis Hughes created this poster for the Interdepartmental War Savings Bond Committee in 1944. His use of detail is excellent—note the wedding band, for instance—and he combines it with a somber, heavily shadowed, monochromatic approach. In this poster, "[the] themes and draftsmanship cross the border into melodrama," Zbynek Zeman wrote. This view of the soldier as gravedigger is certainly unusual and would not have been used earlier in the war.

Riegel here deals with the central controversy about the artistic pretensions of posters. Do the best of the posters rise above their milieu and make timeless statements? Peter Stanley doesn't think so. "Though many respected artists were associated with poster art in both world wars, the war poster is in some ways the opposite of art," he wrote. "Art extends understanding, war posters restrict it. . . . A successful poster is capable of only one interpretation." Given that definition, a poster could never be art.

Is that important? Probably not. And the posters have their eloquent defenders, too. Critic Alan Gowans calls posters "the great repository of arts with social function in and for our time. Here, for all their triviality and banality, are arts which still in fact *do* something, arts that can be evaluated objectively because they have specific objectives." The posters of World War II certainly have specific objectives. If the American people's response and the American military's success are any indication, the verdict is that the posters deserve a few medals of their own.

CARE is costly

BUY WAR BONDS & STAMPS

You can trace the development of the attitudes toward the war in a poster's choice of subject matter. In 1942 and 1943, the predominant tone was upbeat and brash. In this 1945 poster, however, the wounded sergeant's face shows the typical, late war expression: he seems tired and sullen, almost shell-shocked. Adolph Treidler created this poster for the Treasury Department.

Chapter 6

Genres, Symbols, Styles and Techniques

The Weapons on the Wall

Confronted with the cornucopia of posters printed during World War II, you are immediately struck by their amazing variety. They range in quality from fine art to crude illustration, in topic from soldier to farmer to housewife. They are executed in numerous artistic media, in vivid color and somber hues, and trigger emotions from enthusiasm to horror.

Collectors and critics deal with this visual avalanche in two ways. They fit posters into recognized genres based on the target audience or the goal: building morale, warning people about spies and sabotage, or recruiting workers and soldiers. Posters also link together by artistic techniques, and by the artist's use of such elements as humor, symbols, and ethnic stereotypes.

The appearance of variety

As Philip Meggs wrote, "War graphics spanned the spectrum of graphic approaches and quality in a chaotic free-for-all ranging from vigorous modernism to amateurish cartoon treatments." Much of this variety, however, is superficial. At their roots, the posters fall into a handful of well-recognized categories. In the preface to one collection of posters, O. W. Riegel pointed out, "War posters of all countries and times are remarkably similar in their basic messages." In essence, the posters promote enthusiasm among the folks at home, build the morale of the troops, exhort civilians to make sacrifices, and discourage the enemy.

In *War*, Zbynek Zeman selected five groups; all are represented in this book. His first group contains posters that make direct, emotional appeals to patriotism. Zeman called these posters, with their tattered stars-and-stripes and morale-boosting slogans, "the most important category."

Zeman's second group of posters deals with national security by showing the saboteurs and spies that lurk behind innocent citizens and workers. These posters "instruct and exhort," Zeman wrote, and are typified by the "loose lips sink ships" slogan.

The third group concerns the war effort on the home front: complying with the rules about rationing and price controls, conserving scarce materials, finding

No selection of war posters would be complete without war bond posters. This illustration was the cover of an information program distributed for the Sixth War Loan campaign. National Archives.

Previous page
This poster, issued by the Army Service Forces Depots in 1944, is unusual in that it doesn't depict soldiers in actual combat, which was a much more graphic, attractive milieu for the poster artists, since it allowed them to show explosions and gunfire. As a result, it falls outside the common genres of posters.

This literal but effective portrayal of intelligence gathering employs an image that would be familiar to every viewer: putting together a puzzle. National Archives.

a job and showing up every day, and in general backing the attack (supporting the general war effort). This category is the most important—it is certainly the largest and most varied.

Zeman's fourth group contains posters relating to America's allies, showing them to be brave and steadfast, enlisting America's support in both military ways (as in the case of lend-lease war material) and humanitarian ways (as in caring for refugees).

Finally, a small group of posters makes statements about the enemy. These posters tend to vilify and ridicule the enemy. At one extreme, they contain some rare humorous posters produced during the war; at the other, they contain images of horror and atrocity.

These categories are useful when dealing with the printed Niagara of war posters produced during World War II. The collector or critic would be hard put to find a poster that didn't fit into at least one of these slots. Many posters overlap, which makes categorization difficult instead of easy.

"The lift to your chin . . . the grit in your craw"

Morale was an enduring concern of the war, on the battlefront and home front alike. Although the concept is familiar, an exact definition is elusive. Morale is mental, not physical. It includes elements of courage, confidence, discipline and enthusiasm. Soldiers with good morale are brave; soldiers with poor morale are quick to retreat. Citizens with good morale gladly pay taxes and willingly work overtime; citizens with poor morale spread rumors and buy black market pork chops. The word *morale* shares its roots with the word *moral*, and particularly during the war, it had clear-cut overtones of knowing the difference between right and wrong, and the difference between good and evil.

Wartime writers had their own colorful ways of describing the concept. Writing in *America Organizes to Win the War* (1942), Arthur Upham Pope, chairman of the Committee for National Morale, explained, "Morale is the spine in your back, the lift to your chin, the song on your lips, the grit in your craw. Morale is the spirit that makes you say defiantly, 'Is **that** so?' when you are told you aren't man enough to do something— and makes you do it!"

"In a way, the armed forces are only the facade of a nation at war," Pope continued. "That facade must be constantly supported by the beams and girders behind it—and they, in turn, must be held in place by the strong cement of morale. . . . [T]he fighting spirit, the military morale, will fade and die every time the men have

reason to feel that the war effort at home is less than their own. They have to feel that the fighting spirit at home is equal to their own. After all, a man can hardly be expected to face machine guns and dive bombers if he has evidence that the people he is fighting for are whimpering because they have less sugar than usual, or because they haven't any golf balls."

No one doubted that high morale was good. The question was how to raise it and keep it high. Exhibition baseball games for the troops? Glenn Miller and his

Next page
Herbert Morton Stoops created this poster for the OWI in 1944. Zbynek Zeman said this poster "can hardly be called hard-hitting," because he found that the cause and effect are not graphically linked. However, it seems clear that an alleged security leak tipped off enemy ground patrols to expect the paratroopers, with fatal results. The distorted, weird angles of the parachutes and the corpse add a disturbing tone to this poster, as does the green color of the dead paratrooper.

CARELESS TALK
...got there first

93

Previous page
Adolph Treidler created this poster in 1942 for the British and American Ambulance Corps, which issued it as a fund-raiser. Treidler had become well-known during World War I for his work with the Division of Pictorial Publicity.

band at a USO concert? Clean, meaningful hobbies for the folks at home? Juke boxes? Church socials?

Posters offered dozens of suggestions. In *America Organizes to Win the War*, Charles Judd, head of the Department of Education at Chicago University, offered the following suggestions as 1942 morale boosters: "Conservation, study of social problems, labor, and contribution to the public good are to be recommended as ensuring that balanced and calm view of the war which is described by the phrase 'high morale.' People who are constructively occupied do not worry."

Absence of worry was a laudable goal during the war years, but one that was rarely attained. In truth, everyone had plenty to worry about, from rubber shortages to labor unrest to air raids. A predominant

Poster artists never seemed to tire of this theme, producing dozens of iterations. If loose lips had sunk as many ships, shot down as many aircraft and doomed as many patrols as posters claimed, the Allies would have been in deep trouble. National Archives.

headache, according to war posters, was the suspected presence of saboteurs, those rotten apples in the barrel of democracy. Fear of spies triggered a whole genre of "careless talk" posters that were a specialty of World War II. According to historian Lee Kennett, author of *For the Duration*, "Much of this preoccupation [with saboteurs] could be traced back to World War I. . . . [T]he Red Scare which had followed had helped implant the image of the hidden, relentless subversive, boring away at the nation's vital core."

A popular term for this threat was *fifth column*, which initially referred to a global network of German nationals and sympathizers. The term had come into use during the Spanish Civil War (1936–39), when four columns of rebels advanced against Madrid, aided by a "fifth column" of sympathizers within the city. By the summer of 1940, a book titled *The Fifth Column Is Here* was a best seller. It claimed that more than a million fifth columnists were in America.

Other sensationalist, paranoia-inducing exposés hit the commercial market. Hollywood began producing spy movies and continued to do so well into the war. Poster designers didn't lag behind, dealing primarily with information leaks, as well as with sabotage in war industries and even arson. A 1943 poster from the Department of Agriculture's State Forest Service read, "Our carelessness—Their Secret Weapon. Prevent forest fires." It shows Hitler and a Japanese face above a line of burning trees.

The virulence of the fear shows in the extremes to which some posters carried their approach. Anton Otto Fischer's poster captioned "A careless word . . . a needless loss" shows the corpse of a sailor, washed by an angry surf, a shocking image during the early part of the war. John Atherton's 1943 version substituted the words ". . . another cross," with equally grim graphics.

Still other posters of this genre urged the viewer to ignore rumors, which were theoretically spread by foreign agents. For example, in May 1941, a widespread rumor was that nearly half of all ships carrying lend-lease aid were being sunk, when in fact very few were.

Next page
This 1943 poster by John Falter, US Navy Reserve, lacks the usual grim and dismal tone of the "loose lips" genre. The attractive image could almost be used as a recruiting poster.

Page 96
This poster, by Wesley Heyman, is perhaps the sentimental classic of the war. The signature is dated 1943, but the Government Printing Office credit line is 1944. Heyman made this poster for the Joint Security Committee. According to a document in the OWI files, it was "one of the few unsolicited posters that has been used by any government agency. . . . Its aggregate reproduction was in the millions, and OWI reports that requests for it broke all previous records."

If you tell where he's going . . . He may never get there!

ANTON OTTO FISCHER

a careless word...

A NEEDLESS LOSS

98

Henry Sharp Goff, Jr., who used the name Essargee, created this poster in 1942. His bright, simple, cartoonlike technique is vivid and easy to recognize. At various times, soldiers or representatives from all the Axis countries appeared as rats.

Hitler became such a familiar figure that Henry Sharp Goff, Jr., needed to show few features to suggest the archvillain. Early in the war, a Chicago bartender came up with an idea: to organize the United States' 200,000 tavern keepers to fight fires, give first aid and look out for propaganda. He felt bartenders were good at keeping cool in sudden emergencies. Records don't show whether the bartender's brainstorm was adopted. Although the federal government pumped out thousands of posters, many more came from private or commercial sources. This poster was published by the House of Seagram, according to the credit line.

Next page
This excellent illustration was done by Sergeant Tom Lovell. The subtle lighting, the muddy uniform and the marine's serious expression all put it among the best in terms of realistic portrayals. The poster also shows the patches of the 1st and 2nd Marine Divisions, left, and the 1st and 2nd Aircraft Wings, right, the units that were involved in the battle. The poster is dated September 10, 1945. This marine's battered, open-collared uniform is realistic; it contrasts dramatically with some of the dressier, more formal posters produced earlier in the war, when neat uniforms were prescribed. The version of this poster in the War Memorial Museum's collection has a yellow image on the back, showing a woman in uniform in a jeep, with the slogan "Room for you!" This poster may have been discontinued or the printers made a mistake. Either way, the ghostly image is evidence of the campaign to conserve paper.

An extreme result was the internment of Japanese-Americans in California. No American-born Japanese had been caught doing anything subversive, but the authorities interpreted that lack of action as extremely fishy. The Japanese-Americans must have been following orders and biding their time, the authorities figured. As a result, from March through August 1942, more than 100,000 people entered internment camps. Most historians now feel, in retrospect, that this action cannot be justified on the grounds of national security; by paying reparations to the people who were interned, the government has now officially recognized its error. However, it is strong testimony to the mood of the times. In *For the Duration*, Lee Kennett tells about local searches for subversives and spies that got so out of hand that the California State Defense Council issued this order: "Under no circumstances are local defense councils or other local or state civilian defense organizations to conduct investigations relative to espionage, sabotage, or subversive activities."

Guarding against information leaks was something that the folks at home could do, however, and—at least in the world of the poster—they did it with vigor. "The beauty of the 'careless talk' campaign was that people

GUADALCANAL America's World War II ground offensive began Aug. 7, 1942, when the 1st Marine Division, Reenforced, landed at Guadalcanal. Through rivers, swamps and steaming jungle the rugged, resolute Marines fought on until this first great stepping-stone to Japan was won!

PAINTING BY SGT. TOM LOVELL

ENLIST NOW
U.S. MARINE CORPS

Jon Witcomb created this Navy recruiting poster in 1944.

This is another entry in a series of similar posters emphasizing significant battles, campaigns and victories.

This poster is credited to Alpha Litho. Company, Camden, New York. It is signed HHL and dated June 30, 1942. Whereas most posters concentrated on a single theme, this poster touches another base by plugging war bonds as well as recruiting; note the tiny minuteman symbol at left. The albino eagle, which has broken the wing off the clunky Japanese aircraft, is a unique element.

could feel involved in the war, playing a part and combating the enemy, merely by doing nothing and keeping their mouths shut," O. W. Riegel concluded.

Courage and gallantry in action

The opposite of doing nothing was enlisting, and millions of American men and women did just that. The draft ensured that the military got enough people, but for the folks who entered voluntarily, recruiting campaigns produced some of the most memorable, familiar and attractive posters of the war.

At the end of 1941, wrote Donald Rogers in *Since You Went Away*, "the reminders of the war were everywhere. The draft had been accelerated, and soldiers, sailors, marines and coast guardsmen were seen on the streets of every community in the land, and they filled every bus terminal and railroad depot. Every public building had posters, urging young men to enlist, and now there were posters urging young women, too, to get into the nursing corps or to join the Army's WACs or the Navy's WAVES."

Draft-age men and women—and, by extension, all people in America—were supposed to ask themselves this question whenever they looked in their mirror: Are you doing your share? The appeals were creative and diverse. Some emphasized excitement, such as the 1941 Navy poster that said, "'Mosquitoes' . . . dashing through the seas at express train speed, the Navy's PT boats protect our shores and pack a sting. Enlist today—the United States Navy."

The appeals to heroism were potent. Jes William Schlaikjer produced a poster for the War Department in 1943 that announced, "Courage and gallantry in action—infantry, United States Army." It looks like a movie poster, with dramatic lighting played on a realistic, rifle-bearing giant soldier who looms out of a battle

scene, with tanks at his feet, surrounded by smoke and explosions.

An Australian poster by Harry Weston adopted a less grandiose, more personal approach. Weston contrasted a uniformed soldier with an idle young man who is lounging in a lawn chair, smoking and drinking, wearing two-toned shoes, and with a cricket bat propped nearby. "Which picture would your father like to show his friends?" the caption asked.

The recruits poured forth. Six months to the minute after Pearl Harbor, the Navy simultaneously signed up the men who had responded to its call for 10,000 "Avengers of Pearl Harbor." It got 2,000 more than it had requested. By the end of 1942, the Army Air Forces had enlisted between 600,000 and 800,000 men, including 50,000 pilots. The Navy, which had enlisted only 100 pilots per month in May 1940, was signing up 800 per month in July 1941; by January 1942, it was signing up 2,500 per month. At that rate, it was adding 30,000 pilots within a year. All branches of the military continued to issue recruiting posters throughout the war. The Marines, in particular, capitalized on well-known victories during the later years.

Although military recruiting grabbed the spotlight and the headlines, American assembly lines and factories were also engaged in recruiting workers to take the place of the men who had put on uniforms and to support the tremendous expansion that was necessary to meet the needs of the services. During 1941, nearly 5.5 million workers were placed in defense industries by organized recruiting programs, and things were just starting to get heated up at that point.

Shortages of workers continued throughout the war. In 1944, as part of a campaign to find new workers, the Association of American Railroads (AAR) issued 300,000 copies of a poster that was distributed through the Office of War Information and the Office of Defense Transportation. Another massive effort was aimed at recruiting farm workers, as American farmers dramatically expanded the number of acres under cultivation. The increased demands—to ship food to the front lines, to other countries under lend-lease and to refugees in Europe, as well as to feed the folks at home—hit farmers at a time when more and more able-bodied farm hands were putting on khaki and olive-drab uniforms rather than denim overalls.

Once new workers started punching the time clock, supervisors and managers had to try to keep them there. Industrial safety programs were one way to maximize the effectiveness of the work force, and they were necessary because the combination of inexperienced workers and streamlined training programs meant that factories were extremely hazardous. A 1942 War Production Board poster showed grave markers with picks, axes, oilcans and saws leaning against them. Its caption read, "More American workers were killed and wounded in industrial accidents last year than *all* the casualties from bombs in Britain in two years of war. Follow safety rules!"

Industrial posters also discouraged absenteeism and encouraged innovation. One sarcastic poster shows a Tojo-like figure saying thanks to a slacker. The poster

The Army Recruiting and Publicity Bureau produced this poster on August 1, 1943, according to its credit line. The three alleged WACs in the window look suspiciously like starlets, giving this poster the feel of an ad for a television series. Had they seen this poster, lonely GIs on the battlefronts would certainly have had some recommendations about where these WACs were needed.

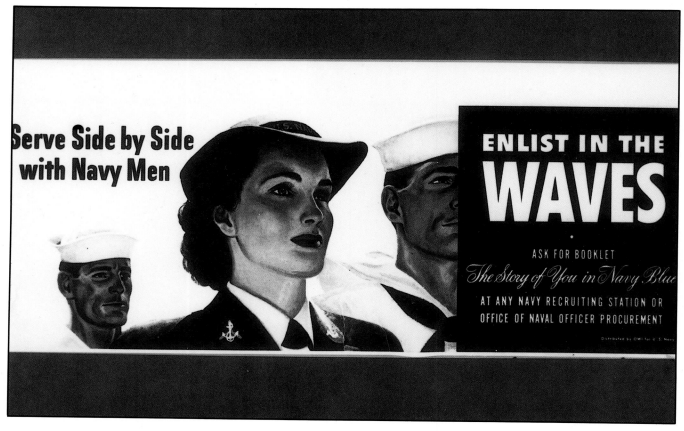

The generals and admirals were willing to accept women into the services, but few polls showed popular civilian support for the idea. Women who heeded the call faced a complex challenge. National Archives.

Sportsmen in the War

This magazine editorial offers a vintage blend of wartime themes and attitudes: concerns about self-defense, incendiary saboteurs, ammo shortages. The tone is serious, but the idea that everyone at home should do as much hunting and fishing as possible in order to maintain their own morale seems a comical stab at making a virtue out of what wasn't even a necessity before the war.

Never before has the sportsman been able to do so much for his country as he is doing today. Everyone can help, but none so much as the man who has kept himself fit through outdoor living, who owns guns and knows how to use them, and who doesn't get panicked when things go wrong. No other single group can offer as much as that.

England learned a bitter lesson two years ago when she found that her civilian population was virtually without arms and the knowledge of how to use them. Her call to American sportsmen for guns and ammunition proved that she sorely needed something that only sportsmen could supply—something she lacked because gun-owning isn't such a simple matter in England as it is in America. We can thank God that we were not in the same fix ourselves when we finally entered the war.

It is not probable that we shall ever have to use our shotguns and rifles for anything but game shooting, but if the time should ever come, they'll be in our gun cabinets where we can reach them in a hurry. We almost lost them a short while ago, and *Hunting and Fishing* is almighty proud right now of the part it played in keeping those guns in the sportmen's homes, where they belong.

England learned another lesson when thousands of her people huddled bravely in bomb shelters while Nazi planes roared overhead in the night. She learned how hard it is to keep a stiff upper lip when things go wrong—and how vitally important it is to do so. Morale, both military and civilian, plays a big part in the winning of a war, and it's good to know that there are twelve million sportsmen in this country who have enough moral fiber—*guts* is a better word for it—to take the good with the bad without panic or jitters.

We know that the morale of our armed forces could be seriously affected if the folks at home became jittery and discouraged. Keeping home was captioned "On the Job for Victory"; it was issued by various companies and agencies (including Texaco).

Short circuits to emotion

Regardless of their themes, posters speak a common language. They share a vocabulary and techniques that recur through decades of changing purposes. Studying the posters of World War I, O. W. Riegel found certain recurrent strategies: images of or quotes from national leaders, past and present; symbols (a cross, flag, eagle, lion or snake), which Riegel calls short circuits to emotion; slogans; and caricatures that ridicule the foe. Many of these techniques recur in the poster of the Second World War, as well, with the addition of more modern symbols—aircraft kill markings, for example.

The classic example of the American poster symbol from World War I is Lady Liberty, brandishing the sword of justice and carrying the torch of freedom. In a poster by J. C. Leyendecker, for instance, a Boy Scout kneels, holding a huge sword up to the outstretched hand of the classical figure known alternatively as Columbia or Miss Liberty, who stands behind him, holding a shield. "USA Bonds—Third Liberty Loan

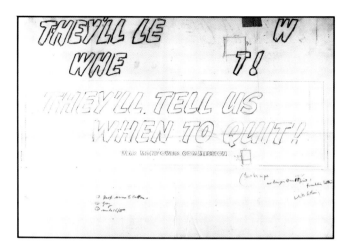

This preliminary sketch shows that the artist considered two versions of the slogan. National Archives.

Next page
McClelland Barclay did this inspiring poster for the Navy. Is it any wonder young men heeded this wild-blue-yonder call?

morale high is one job that every last fisherman and hunter can do better than the next fellow. For no other reason than that, we should plan to fish and hunt this year as much as we can—to keep ourselves physically and mentally fit for the big part we are playing in the war.

The war effort today calls for volunteers for air raid warden service, emergency police and firemen, home guardsmen and a multitude of other services that are vitally essential to our security. Here again the sportsman is the man for the job. Alert, quick to act in emergency, able to take care of himself, he makes the ideal man to assume responsibility. As forest patrolmen, guarding the woods against incendiary saboteurs, woodsmen are worth a dozen men who are not at home in the wilderness.

Still another great contribution sportsmen are making is in the efficiency of our armed forces. As this is being written, guerilla warfare in Russia is wreaking havoc on the headlong Nazi retreat from the Moscow area. The deadly efficiency of the Russian guerilla is attributed directly to the fact that those fighters are as familiar with guns as American sportsmen are themselves. It is not coincidence that the sharp-shooting Russians have been one of the largest buyers of American-made .22 ammunition in recent years. The Russian success in crushing the Nazi war machine should be all the proof we need of the value of our thousands of rifle ranges and skeet fields.

One-fifth of the selectees who are now fighting for their country, or who are now in training camps learning how to fight, are sportsmen. We can't help thinking what a pleasant surprise it must have been to the range officers at Devens, Edwards, Dix, Bragg and Benning when some of their rookies grabbed a Springfield or Garand and began to pour .30 calibre slugs into the target like veterans. Those sharp-shooting rookies were the fellows we've been hunting with; the fellows who have been shooting up hundreds of thousands of rounds of smallbore ammunition in their cellars and at club ranges, and wearing paths around our skeet fields. And if we don't miss our guess, those are the fellows who are going to pull a lot of weight now that the chips are down and the lead has started to fly.

But to win the war we shall need more than the firepower of sportsmen—more than an ample supply of tanks and guns and battleships. Victory will come only as the spirit of the people wills it, on the production line, in the home, at our every-day jobs. It is here that the sportsman will make his greatest contribution. Not just the five and one-half million hunters who aren't in the army, but also all the fishermen who aren't hunters and the campers who neither hunt nor fish; these are the Americans whose high morale will count when the going gets tough. They are the ones whose refusal to become jittery, whose sacrifice and resourcefulness, and appreciation of the civil liberties at stake will make them leaders in their own communities and a force of unity throughout the country.

All sportsmen can be proud today for all they can do to serve their country in its time of great need. By the same token, the publishers of *Hunting and Fishing* are proud, too, for the privilege of serving America's great army of sportsmen.—The Editors

From Hunting & Fishing *magazine, February 1942.*

Attention!

The attention of all young men, who
are citizens of the United States, is
invited to the advantages incident to
enlistment in the United States Navy.

AGE LIMITS 18 AND UNDER 31

See the nearest Recruiting Officer

The wartime shortage of workers wasn't gender specific. This poster, OWI poster number 52, was issued in 1943.

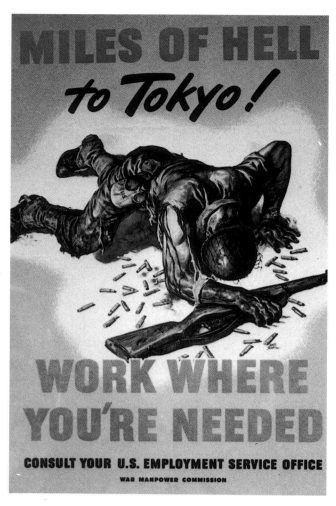

Amos Sewell originally made this poster for the American Fat Salvage Committee, sometime before June 1944. The War Manpower Commission adapted it and issued it in 1945.

Campaign—Boy Scouts of America—Weapons for Liberty," the captions say. The sword has the motto "Be prepared" on its blade.

Along with Uncle Sam, the American eagle was Lady Liberty's counterpart during World War II. The fierce bird was already a familiar and beloved symbol, as evidenced by a passage from a speech given by President Roosevelt on February 23, 1942. Talking about people who believed in "self-imposed isolation," Roosevelt said, "Those Americans who believed that we could live under the illusion of isolationism wanted the American eagle to imitate the tactics of the ostrich.

Previous page
The artist who painted this view of sunset flight operations—Matt Murphey—was in the Navy. The carrier looks relatively modern; the biplane doesn't.

Next page
Sergeant Tom Lovell's realistic view of the flag raising on Iwo Jima was used by the War Finance Division of the Treasury Department, on the occasion of the Seventh War Loan in 1945. The poster shows the patches of the Marine units involved in the battles on Iwo Jima: top to bottom, V Marine Amphibious Corps, 3rd Marine Division, 4th Marine Division, 5th Marine Division and 4th Aircraft Wing. Compared with another artist's version of this scene in the "Now, All Together" poster, this one shows a more horizontal flagstaff, uniform pants and jackets that don't match, and a more colorful and prominent rifle.

Page 112
Captain Vic Guinness created this poster in 1945. The poster shows the patches of the V Marine Amphibious Corps, 2nd Marine Division, 4th Marine Division and 4th Aircraft Wing. The oriental arch and palm trees add a sort of travelogue air to this scene. Tinian and Saipan are part of the Mariana Islands.

115

Previous page
This slogan plays on the phrase "to hold," meaning don't cash in your bonds. It is identified "Official U.S. Treasury Poster/WFD [War Finance Division] 891." The OWI archives have a piece of correspondence about this poster, from James Herbert, the New York art director for OWI, to Jacques DunLany, chief of OWI's Division of Poster Clearance, dated Feb. 1, 1944. In his note, Herbert said, "Apparently the 'To Have and To Hold' poster has not been licked yet. I am hoping the present very rough sketch will bring this closer to solution, if only by the process of elimination. It is pointed out that the use of the flag on the field is against regulations. Perhaps you will get a clarifying decision on this. I think the upward rush toward the flag and the general movement in the 28" long poster has some advantages." Apparently, the problems were solved.

Albert Dorne did this poster in 1944. Note the wavy lines at the snake's tail indicating motion—an unusual, cartoonish technique. Dorne started his career doing illustrations for sheet music covers and his illustrations appeared in many major magazines in the thirties and forties. He was later president of the Society of Illustrators and earned the first Gold Medal from the New York Art Directors Club.

116

the war, a December entry said, "One of the stars on our service flag now represents a boy who is 'missing in action.' And two of my close friends have now lost sons in the South Pacific. Quite suddenly the machine guns are chattering where I can hear them."

A passage in Donald Rogers' book *Since You Went Away* mentioned that "service flags hung in millions of windows, a star for each son at war." If every family had posted its flag, nearly 8 million of them would have been hung in 1942 and another 4 million in the next two years. The service flag in the White House window had four stars.

Famous faces—which ranged from the political to the mythological—were other popular elements of posters, as were well-known victories. British World War I posters featured St. George and the Duke of Wellington. An American counterpart, which encouraged American women to buy war savings stamps, showed Joan of Arc, sword upraised, a beam of light behind her head. A poster for the Community War Fund, titled "Give a Virginian's Share," showed Robert E. Lee and George Washington in the background, looming over the helmeted head of a soldier. Winston Churchill frequently starred in British posters; in one photomontage, he smiles as Hurricane fighters circle his hat and firing tanks surround his feet. The caption says, "Go Forward Together." On the American side of the Atlantic, Dwight Eisenhower, Franklin Roosevelt and Chester Nimitz were usually cast in the starring role.

Less specifically famous but even more ubiquitous in posters is the simple image of the generic hero, nearly always a soldier during the war, a figure who rarely varied even between warring countries. As described by Denis Judd in *Posters of World War II*, "Archetypal heroes fix the middle distance with keen (and generally blue) eyes; their square jaws and brawny forearms transcend loyalties and ideologies." In general, both men and women, in posters (and even more in advertisements), were overwhelmingly Caucasian in appearance.

Poster makers were creative when it came to depicting the enemy. If there were several ways to show heroes, there were dozens of ways to show a louse. The extreme Allied attitude toward Hitler—and by extension, every weapon-toting enemy—was summed up by Winston Churchill, in a speech broad-

Next page
Georges Schreiber made this poster in 1943, although the signature says "42."

Page 118
This poster was made by Dean Cornwell in 1945. Cornwell was from Louisville, Kentucky. He painted murals, illustrated books and magazines, and was a Work Projects Administration (WPA) artist. This illustration contains a $200 bond.

118

cast on June 22, 1941, after the Nazi invasion of Russia: "Hitler is a monster of wickedness, insatiable in his lust for blood and plunder. Not content with having all Europe under his heel or else terrorized in various forms of abject submission, he must now carry his work of butchery and desolation among the vast multitudes of Russia and of Asia. The terrible military machine which we and the rest of the civilized world so foolishly, so supinely, so insensately allowed the Nazi gangsters to build up year by year from almost nothing; this machine cannot stand idle, lest it rust or fall to pieces."

In European posters, Hitler was shown as a monster. Curiously, in American posters, he is more often ridiculed. Once he became an inhabitant of American posters, Hitler found himself transformed into a rat, a gorilla and a hyena. The practice of using ethnic stereotypes in posters was well established, with ample precedent during World War I. To communicate the concept of Germans, a 1915 Australian poster showed

Next page
This poster comes from a cover painting for the Saturday Evening Post, *the magazine for which Norman Rockwell first began doing covers in 1916. The poster deserves an award for emotional symbols per square inch, including the shy girlfriend, the cheerful puppy and the curious neighbors. It depicts more service flags than does any other poster of the war.*

Page 121
Ike was a natural choice for this 1944 war bond appeal. Although he had little reputation as a battlefield general early in the war, he climbed the military totem pole as a staff specialist or coordinator and was chosen to lead the Anglo-American invasion forces in North Africa in early 1943, linking up with Sir Bernard Montgomery's army to end Axis resistance in that theater and taking 750,000 prisoners. Artist of this poster Boris Chaliapin was a poster designer from New York City. The poster was marked WFD 936.

This display, in a Washington building identified as the Tempo V building, includes a pair of well-known posters, and a picture of nighttime farming at center. The set of posters at bottom touches most of the big bases: security, second from left; war bonds, third and fifth from left; rationing, center; and conservation, right. Gordon Parks made this photo for the Office of War Information in March 1942. Library of Congress.

Previous page
C. C. Beall produced this poster in 1945. Beall was an illustrator for Collier's *and* American *magazines. The poster was based on the famous Associated Press photo that rapidly came to symbolize victory, the Marine Corps spirit and the turning tide of the war. Writing about the photo for the* Washington Post *on March 12, 1945, war correspondent Shirley Povich enthused, "You've seen it, as who hasn't—the thrill-picture of the war thus far; that camera shot with all the beauty of a sculpture piece showing seven U.S. Marines silhouetted against the Pacific sky as they plant the American flag on Mount Suribachi's crest. At headquarters here they're calling it the greatest flag picture since Washington crossing the Delaware. They say you'll see it on the Nation's calendars for generations to come." In Povich's account, photographer Joe Rosenthal told of spending half an hour climbing the 550 foot mountain and said the Marines waited to plant the flag until Rosenthal had piled up some rocks and sandbags so that he could get the full picture. In this artist's treatment, the uniforms are muted and all the same color, which makes the soldiers almost look like statues.*

Alfred Charles Parker created this poster in 1942. Parker was a leading illustrator for women's magazines by the mid thirties, working for Cosmopolitan, Ladies' Home Journal *and* Woman's Home Companion. *Note that an Army service cap is lying on the floor in the right foreground. The poster is credited, "Illustration courtesy of Ladies Home Journal."*

"the Hun" as identical to the barbarians who sacked ancient Rome. An American poster from World War I by H. R. Hopps was captioned, "Destroy this mad brute." "The Hun" on this poster was shown as a yellow-fanged gorilla with moustache and spiked helmet, holding a bare-breasted woman in one arm and a club that says "kultur" in the other, standing on a shoreline that says "America."

This transformation didn't always meet with popular approval. One series of World War I Australian posters, which portrayed a German as a blood-stained ogre grasping the globe, drew protests in Australia's parliament. One representative called the posters "repulsive pictorial incitements to bloodshed," reported Peter Stanley in *What Did You Do in the War, Daddy?*

Nevertheless, insulting stereotypes were a necessary part of how people come to terms with the death splurge that accompanies modern war. Compared to the Japanese, the Germans got off easy. Hideki Tojo degenerated to a pair of slanted eyes and huge buckteeth. As Paul Fussell observed in *Wartime*, "[War is] a political, social, and psychological disaster; it is also a perceptual and rhetorical scandal from which total recovery is unlikely. . . . [S]oldiers and civilians alike reduce [the world] to a simplified sketch featuring a limited series of classifications into which people, in the process dehumanized and deprived of individuality or eccentricity, are fitted."

"If the Japanese were type-cast as animals of an especially dwarfish but vicious species, the Germans were recognized to be human beings, but of a perverse type, cold, diagrammatic, pedantic, unimaginative, and thoroughly sinister," Fussell continued.

The folks at home were saturated with these images. "When Americans went to the movies they saw a newsreel, which outside the major centers had to consist of rather timeless news because it took a number

Next page
Signed Bingham, possibly James R. Bingham, this poster was produced for the Sixth War Loan in 1944. This grim, salty, unshaven soldier is a far cry from the statuesque, overly handsome models that appeared on some early recruiting posters.

Page 125
This 1943 poster is credited, "Official U.S. Army Poster." The presence of blood on the soldier's sleeve marks an early appearance of graphic wounds in war posters. Nevertheless, the soldier's statuesque pose, strong physique and hearty demeanor indicate he is healthy and feeling good. The soldier's coloring is odd—he seems to be covered with dust, or even made of clay—particularly compared with the vivid red of the flag, which, since it is the enemy's, has been reduced to a mere souvenir. The artist was Ronald McLeod.

123

124

125

of days to get the film distributed," Donald Rogers wrote. "Most such ten-minute features were saturated with propaganda, managing to leave the audience with the impression that the Japanese were subhuman and the Nazis were inhuman and that only total extermination of both breeds would permit the survival of the decent people in the free world."

With such psychological and pictorial extremes on one end, it is not surprising that humorous posters were rare. As Zbynek Zeman observed in *Selling the War*, "Patriotic posters have little place for humor. Their message is grand, sometimes pompous; exclamation marks at the end of slogans are frequent." Amidst this pomposity, it is a relief to find a little poster such as the one drawn by Vernon Grant, which showed a cartoon soldier diving into a pool and getting stung in his bare

butt by a mosquito. "Fight the peril behind the lines," the caption warned. "Keep covered from sundown to sunrise." The soldiers, in the end, usually had more practical concerns.

Next page
This poster is produced by General Motors Corporation (GMC) in 1941. A small oval inset at the lower right corner shows a GMC truck towing a field howitzer. The slogan at the bottom edge is one of dozens of similar wartime phrases: "Keep 'em pulling for victory." Many poster campaigns developed and used similar slogans, as did civilian companies.

Page 129
This poster was produced by the Oldsmobile Division of General Motors Corporation in 1942. One reference gives the artist's name as Swasey, although the poster is undated and unsigned.

"Wait . . . It's too soon for careless talk"

This internal memorandum from the Office of War Information was dated April 11, 1945.
J.D.H. to J.D.L.

Careless talk campaign coming up, and J.D.L. would like Art Directors to work on it.

Japs are increasing their intelligence operations. In this country, following VE Day in Europe, there will be a complete black out. No one will know where anybody is until they hit in the Pacific. [We] want civilians to cooperate in that black out. The new slogan will be:
"WAIT . . . IT'S TOO SOON FOR CARELESS TALK"
5 or 6 copies coming up tonight in courier of copy. We want a complete new trade mark—Helguera's is out.

Suggestions:
    1-Hour glass with rising sun behind it.
    2-Grimy looking soldier in Pacific.
Sketches need not be more than 2" high.
They should be in Fri. night and put in courier.
The symbol should not be a toothy caricature of a Jap. The reason: There is so much of that, that there is no more real power.

6 mos. before B-29 was removed from secret list, or even heard of in this country, the Japs knew about them—what they were for and every technical detail about them, thus destroying its initial use. These plans were found on the Japs in Burma in 1944.

The Security of War Information heads this Campaign.

Good news from home
TANKS
PLANES
GUNS
SHIPS
MORE PRODUCTION
WAR PRODUCTION BOARD – A6

Chapter 7

Roots of the War Poster

A Brief History

The history of the poster has been recounted by numerous historians and critics, in lush artistic detail and with extensive expertise. You can certainly enjoy war posters without knowing anything about Jules Cheret, Alphonse Mucha, James Montgomery Flagg, the Office of War Information or the cultural trends of the early forties. However, you probably can't *understand* the posters or appreciate their reasons for existence. A brief history may help the modern viewer realize where posters came from, and it may be invaluable because the modern trend in war posters—namely, that they are very expensive and are gobbled up by collectors for private collections or viewing—is contrary to the wartime use and the ostensible meaning of the posters themselves.

War posters have ancient ancestors and many cousins. According to graphics writer Marion Muller in the Spring 1990 issue of *U&lc,* "The poster is the oldest propaganda tool in history—a relative, only once-removed from Egyptian wall paintings." Early posters included garish playbills for the theater and the circus, auction notices and wanted posters—simple, often

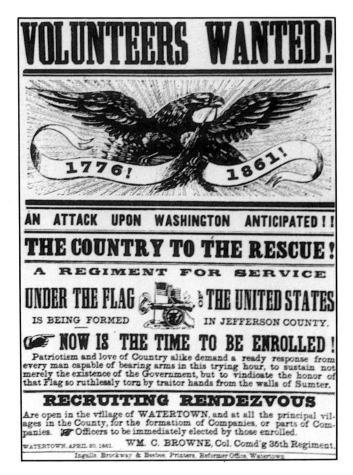

Poster or sign? Or a broadside, which was a large sheet paper printed with political messages or advertising? This poster, from April 1861, looks much like the newspapers of the time, with its dense text, display headlines in various fonts and simple line illustrations. It calls for volunteers to "vindicate the honor of that Flag so ruthlessly torn by traitor hands from the walls of Sumter"; as usual, posters have no place for debate or for objective description. Library of Congress.

Previous page
A well-known artist from World War II, Stevan Dohanos, created this poster for the War Production Board in 1942; the information line on the poster identifies it as WPB-A6. Dohanos did his first published work in McCall's at age twenty-seven in 1934 and began working for the Saturday Evening Post in 1943, producing more than 120 cover paintings between 1943 and 1959. He also designed twenty-five postage stamps for the US government. During the war, he did at least two "careless talk" posters, another poster for the WPB and a poster for the War Food Administration. Although Dohanos' drawing technique is excellent, this poster's central image of a too-happy soldier is almost generic. Minus the caption, the viewer would have no idea of the topic of the poster. The soldier could well be counting how many days of liberty he had left or the girlfriends he was leaving behind.

graphic public notices aimed at conveying specific information to pedestrians. Therefore, the poster is related to commercial signs on buildings and stores, especially when those signs are more than words, as well as flyers and handouts, commercial and noncommercial paintings on walls, art prints and stand-up display advertisements.

In the definition that was in use during the two world wars, a poster is made of paper; is cheaply produced (unlike art prints); usually combines text and image; is meant to be posted in a public place, as opposed to on a museum, gallery or living room wall; and is meant to persuade viewers to take some action or change some idea.

The poster exists in the netherworld between art and advertisement, flitting back and forth between the extremes. With the invention of lithography in 1798, the stage was set for a new medium that could escape from the world of formal portraits and marble sculpture. By

Time had been standing still in this general store in Chacon, Mora County, New Mexico, in January 1943. These posters from World War I had never been taken down. The American eagle, top, remained a popular icon in posters of the Second World War. The diaphanous vision of the woman, bottom, changed radically into something much more practical and worldly, however, as real-life women picked up wrenches and clipboards. John Collier made this photo for the Office of War Information. Library of Congress.

132

1848, it was possible to print 10,000 sheets per hour. Posters were relatively common in the mid 1800s.

What images and messages were on the posters? All sorts of things, ranging from fine art at one extreme to strident advertisements at the other. O. W. Riegel says the poster "led to an unprecedented democratization and diffusion of art at a time of industrialization and rapid population growth." Lithography was also an excellent tool for reaching the rapidly increasing number of consumers. In the hands of advertisers, lithographed posters were a "union of technology and salesmanship" that went hand in hand with mass production.

Most texts begin the story of posters with an artist named Jules Cheret in Paris, where his posters began to first appear in 1869. Cheret combined the techniques of book-illustration lithography and elements of classic painting with the popular vernacular of the times. The result, plastered on the plain walls of the city, appeared to be a potent new form of art. In time, the walls of posters came to be known as the art gallery of the street, to the extent that fans peeled Cheret's posters from the walls and carried them home.

Prominent European artists—including such names as T. A. Steinlen, Pierre Gavarni, Henri de Toulouse-Lautrec and Alphonse Mucha—began to work in the genre, creating what is now called the art poster. The craze for art posters soon spread to the United States, creating wide-open opportunities for leading American artists. Bicycle manufacturers and magazines were the first to use the posters, the former as commercials and the latter as covers, particularly Edward Penfield's series for *Harper's Magazine*.

Between 1893 and 1896, the poster boom enjoyed what John Barnicoat (in *A Concise History of Posters*) called a "brief yet meteoric rise during which time the American public collected whatever was printed." High-quality printing companies turned out special editions especially for collectors. Formal exhibitions of posters were presented in Paris and in New York. This frenzied collecting was an aberration rather than a rule, however. By 1900, enthusiasm had waned.

Summing up the period from 1870 to World War I, Barnicoat wrote that "posters in general reflected fashionable styles of decoration or spoke the language most likely to appeal to all."

Skipping temporarily over World War I, we next find posters flaring up in Europe in the twenties, this time as the communication medium of choice for political outsiders, protesters and revolutionary groups. Since broadcasting and films were still being developed, "German and other European propagandists were still traveling light in terms of the technical equipment at their disposal," Zbynek Zeman wrote. "In the absence of other media, posters—in Germany and elsewhere—played the key role in political campaigning," he continued. Posters were used by political parties during election campaigns and for party recruiting.

"Serious" artists continued to dabble in posters, often injecting elements of the sort that art critics are fond of identifying. Texts trace, for example, the influence of the art nouveau movement before World War I and of surrealism from the twenties until the end of World War II. In both instances, posters maintained commercial uses as well as decorative ones. Historians agree that the commercial poster had two golden ages, the twenties and thirties and the fifties. And the urge to collect posters, including posters related to such themes as travel, movies and art exhibits, has flared up at different times.

However, what is of interest to us here is the poster's "power to inform and persuade," which John Garrigan points out was "firmly established in times of crisis"—notably the First World War. To be fully functional, Dore Ashton adds, "the poster must have an immediacy of an occasion and a place." Surveying the history of posters, Ashton finds that immediacy in the midthirties, during the Depression, when artists who had rejected the poster as a commercial medium suddenly began to accept it as a powerful instrument of social change.

Jumping briefly past World War II, we find that posters enjoyed another boom in the United States during the flower-power, antiwar sixties—a decade that John Garrigan called "the most innovative and diverse in the history of the poster in [the United States]." Psychedelic posters, like reproductions of war posters, are more decorative than functional, however. The posters of wartime weren't meant to brighten up walls. They had serious business to attend to.

Both world wars produced Niagaras of posters. Critical opinion about the relative merits and the quality of each era of posters is widely divergent.

Before the United States entered World War I, George Creel, a magazine journalist in New York, wrote to President Woodrow Wilson, calling the war "a plain publicity proposition, a vast enterprise in salesmanship, the world's greatest adventure in advertising." Creel became executive secretary of the Committee on Public Information during the war and remained a powerful proponent of what he called "the importance of pictorial publicity in building morale, arousing the spiritual forces of the nation, and stimulating the war will of the people." As quoted in Pierce Fredericks' *The Great Adventure*, Creel said that America didn't need just posters, "it needed the best posters ever drawn." He created the Division of Pictorial Publicity "for those unable or unwilling to read or listen."

When the United States entered the war, graphic artists throughout the country began producing propaganda. Art schools established classes in poster design and contributed thousands of poster designs to official causes. Famous artists also enlisted in the cause, including J. C. Leyendecker, who would eventually do more than 300 covers for the *Saturday Evening Post*.

Starting in April 1917, leading illustrators and designers in the New York area, organized by Charles Dana Gibson, produced about 700 posters in nineteen months. The Navy also had organized volunteers. Some fifty different agencies active in the war—interested in

BEWARE
—OF—
FEMALE SPIES

Women are being employed by the enemy to secure information from Navy men, on the theory that they are less liable to be suspected than male spies. Beware of inquisitive women as well as prying men.

SEE EVERYTHING
HEAR EVERYTHING
SAY NOTHING
Concerning any matter bearing upon the work of the Navy

SILENCE IS SAFETY

This simple, broadside-style poster is from World War I. The "silence is safety" theme would reappear in hundreds of renditions during the Second World War. Most people were still not deluged with striking images all day long, so even this simple effort may have been effective. Naval Historical Center.

recruiting soldiers and sailors, selling liberty bonds and collecting blood—printed an estimated 2,000 to 3,000 posters, and printings of 100,000 were common. The resulting tally was in the millions. According to Clarence Hornung and Fridolf Johnson, authors of *200 Years of American Graphic Art*, "It was the poster artist's finest hour, marked by some of the greatest and most famous posters of all time."

O. W. Riegel, who was a propaganda analyst for the Office of War Information during World War II and later head of the journalism department at Washington and Lee University in Virginia, wrote that World War I marked the "first large-scale use of the poster for political purposes" and served governments as "a primary instrument for mobilizing their peoples for war."

Part of the reason posters were so necessary was that World War I involved the civilian population as well as the military, unlike earlier battles and wars. Critics tend to agree that posters from the First World War had more impact than those of the Second World War, because they had less competition.

According to Zbynek Zeman, "First World War posters were some of the most effective of all the propaganda materials churned out by the war." The Lord Horatio Kitchener "Your Country Needs You!" poster is a classic. On the other hand, author Peter Stanley found the British posters of World War I to be naive, amateur, wordy, homely and hackneyed. Those qualities are predictable, he said, because the posters were usually designed by commercial tradesmen, not artists, who were used to producing advertisements.

Dore Ashton wrote that Pablo Picasso enjoyed looking at posters and old signs, comparing them to wine, which he liked to drink. "The wine available to Americans before the Second World War was often of pretty poor vintage," Ashton wrote. Why? Because American cities, unlike Paris or London, "failed to produce the kinds of spaces conducive to the art of the poster." The United States lacked cafes and kiosks, and billboards were always commercial.

John Barnicoat's verdict on military posters produced between 1870 and 1919 makes a clear link between the commercial origins of posters. "Advertising for war was considered in terms of commercial advertising," he wrote. After the war, "the various political upheavals in Russia and elsewhere determined a new direction for the political poster. This change, however, was not appreciated by many governments— or even by those producing poster designs." As a result, some posters were still simply forms of "commercial persuasion" or an "'artistic' form of advertisement."

Poster critics and collectors argue about which war generated "better" posters, in terms of either artistic technique or overall design. Commercial printers produced some of the less memorable posters of World War I; commercial designers and copywriters from the advertising field turned out some slick ones during World War II. Amateurs and professionals alike produced posters during both wars. In the 1930s, several internationally known artists, including A. M. Cassandre and Jean Carlu from France, left Europe. "The masters of the modern European poster arrived in America during the 1930s and the early 1940s as part of this exodus seeking sanctuary in 'the citadel of democracy,'" wrote Philip Meggs in the November/December 1989 issue of *Print* magazine. One of Carlu's

The posters of World War I and World War II aren't interchangeable, as one critic argues, but themes and techniques do recur. This poster derives from French posters of World War I. "On les aura" was a French revolutionary slogan of 1792. It means "We'll get them," and it was echoed in the First and Second World Wars, each time with new accretions of historical association and sentiment. The original poster was created by Jules Abel Faivre in 1916 for the French 2nd National Defense Loan. It showed a determined soldier moving energetically forward, rifle in right arm, left arm upraised, looking back over his right shoulder, in a classic follow-me-boys pose. A couple American versions were made. This one, produced by the OWI in 1943, has been Americanized by borrowing the famous slogan of John Paul Jones. It is identified on the back as OWI poster number 62. The list of battle locations is chronological, and although the viewer might expect it to be a list of victories, the perspective of 1943 was different than that of two years later. Bataan, along with Corregidor, symbolized the loss of the Philippines in March and April of 1942. At the Coral Sea in May 1942, the Japanese won a tactical victory but were stopped from invading Australia. At Midway in June, the American fleet brought the Japanese to a stop, sinking four Japanese carriers. The fighting opened on Thursday, June 4. Friday's headlines said, "Fleets Clash in Pacific, Great Naval Battle in Progress." The last minor blows of the battle occurred on Saturday, and the radio and press reported Nimitz's message: "A stupendous naval victory is in the making." Guadalcanal, in August, was the first Allied land offensive, the first major amphibious assault and the first major Japanese land defeat. New Guinea was a representative step in the middle of the American island-hopping sweep through the Japanese-held Pacific. Casablanca, Algiers and Tunisia were part of Operation Torch, November 1942, in North Africa.

YOU CAN LICK RUNAWAY PRICES

YOU HOLD THE 7 KEYS TO HOLD DOWN PRICES

 1. Buy and hold War Bonds.

 2. Pay willingly our share of taxes.

 3. Provide adequate life insurance and savings for our future.

 4. Reduce our debts as much as possible.

 5. Buy only what we need and make what we have last longer.

 6. Follow ration rules and price ceilings.

 7. Cooperate with our Government's wage stabilization program.

Distributed by O.W.I. for the Office of Economic Stabilization

135

Previous page
James Montgomery Flagg created this poster in 1944 for the US Office of Economic Stabilization, part of the "Seven Keys to Victory" series aimed at combating inflation. Flagg was prolific in both wars, having produced forty-six posters in World War I. This one, with its text-heavy message and pedantic tone, is not one of his most inspired, and his Uncle Sam seems to have aged. The message about taxes—"Pay willingly our share"—was particularly apropos, however. In 1929, 4 million people filed tax returns. By 1941, to meet the needs of lend-lease and national preparedness, 26 million people were filing returns. By spring 1942, that total had risen to 30 million people, and at the end of 1942, another 5 million had been added. By 1945, 50 million people were wrangling with tax forms and cursing April 15. The Internal Revenue Service had entered the consciousness of the person in the street.

posters, "America's Answer! Production," won the New York Art Directors Club Medal. The bold, simple poster showed a gloved hand using a wrench to turn the letter *o* in the word *production*.

Although the posters of the later world war tended to be more professional, some critics find them to be more prosaic. Peter Stanley said that British posters of World War II "conveyed a strong sense of the commonplace," and their tone was "one of determination rather than bravado."

Another critic finds the posters of World War II to be more realistic, more humorous and "less earnest." The posters from World War I aimed at a general channeling of national feeling; they tended to present the war as a crusade rather than a political and military phenomenon. Posters of World War II required many more specific actions, especially of civilians.

From the perspective of artistic quality, John Barnicoat said, "the posters produced during the Second World War did not add anything to the achievements already established in the development of the poster design generally."

To some extent, themes recur. O. W. Riegel went so far as to say that he felt many posters from the two wars were interchangeable, a statement that is true only for a few of the genres, such as war bond appeals and patriotism. During World War II, posters made a much wider range of appeals for production and conservation. Women were no longer clothed in flowing, ethereal gowns but were "trimmer and more businesslike." Also, posters during World War II contained more elements of caricature, more humor and a more realistic view of combat. They served much more often as simple announcements and as publicity for programs and drives.

The posters of World War II changed during the course of the war. In this change, writer Paul Fussell traces what he calls "the inexorable progress from light to heavy duty." A 1942 poster bearing the caption "we're on God's side" shows Joe Louis, charging for-

ward toward the viewer. He has a long, slim bayonet (soon replaced by a shorter, stocky version that proved more effective) attached to a Springfield rifle. "He wears a clean field jacket, properly buttoned. We half expect a necktie," Fussell wrote. "But a year later who is on God's side seems no longer to matter much, for now open depictions of corpses begin to displace considerations of moral right." Later posters show a drowned American sailor in the surf and a dead paratrooper hanging in the air, with blood on his jacket and hand. By 1945, a poster shows "the awkward, ugly cadaver of a tank crewman sprawled amidst realistically messy battle detritus," Fussell wrote. "Unlike Joe Louis's field jacket, this man's is rumpled and torn, covered with spots of dirt—or blood." The poster says, "This happens every three minutes. Stay on the job and get it over."

A major difference between the posters of the two wars is that photography came into use during the Second World War. Part of the reason for this has to do with trends in design, apart from the war's subject matter. John Barnicoat quoted from the 1941 annual report of the New York Art Directors Association, which said, "The flat 'European' poster technique has been more and more discarded in favour of a three-dimensional rendering. Color photography, photomontage and the airbrush have helped streamline the American poster. . . . Realistic-naturalistic posters are by far in the majority, with only an occasional modern, abstract or symbolic design here or there." That summary would hold true for war posters in general.

In 1942, the OWI issued a poster that featured a cutout photo of Hitler with his mouth open. "'We shall soon have our storm troopers in America!'—Hitler. What do you say, America?" the caption challenged. A 1943 OWI poster showed a photo of a Nazi book burning. "Ten years ago: The Nazis burned these books . . . but free Americans can still read them!" the caption said. Only a harsh, black-and-white photo could do justice to some subjects.

Posters of the earlier world war tended to use much more text than those of the later world war, although exceptions exist. A typical World War I poster was headlined "Remember the Lusitania!" It had no picture, only text. The left-hand column luridly described a mother whose three children, ages six years, four years and six months, died in the sinking. The right-hand column contained clips from German newspapers that celebrated the sinking, mentioning "joyful pride" and "riotous scenes of jubilation." This extreme use of copy is unknown during World War II.

Next page
The "careless word" theme appeared in numerous series and depicted several theaters of war. This version, by Anton Otto Fischer in 1942, was OWI poster number 24. It is among the more colorful and dramatic posters. Later in the war, the tables would be turned: the Allies sunk more than 4 million tons of Japanese shipping in 1944.

A careless word...

...A NEEDLESS SINKING

138

Previous page
This poster was produced in 1944 for the Navy's Industrial Incentive Division. It is particularly interesting for two reasons. First, it combines an unusual photomontage technique with the elements of traditional posters. Second, it reveals the presence of black sailors alongside white sailors in an inset photo. In the drawing, a sailor mans machine guns aboard a landing craft. The photos show the bridge of a ship, a sailor using a semaphore, an aviation gunner and a pilot manning his aircraft. Note the aircraft going down in smoke in the background, a frequent element in posters.

By the Second World War, the poster wasn't the only game in town, propaganda-wise. Broadcasting had taken over as a leading medium for both sides, joining newspapers, leaflets, public loudspeakers and films. The leaflet, a sort of miniposter, was extremely useful. Posters were mainly restricted to territory under a government's control. Leaflets, however, could be injected into another country. Another plus was that they could be two-sided. Like posters, leaflets had to be easy to understand, striking in appearance and able to draw attention quickly.

Even with the emphasis on broadcasting, halfway into the twentieth century people still had no effective way to communicate with the mass of the public. For radio broadcasts to be effective, listeners had to have electricity and radios, and most newspapers and other printed matter had comparatively limited circulations. The poster still had a crucial role to play.

The posters of World War II played their role extremely well. Zbynek Zeman wrote, "From 1943, the Allies started winning propaganda battles as well as military ones. . . . [T]he main tenor of British propaganda was epitomized by the speeches of Churchill: hard-bitten and cautious, gloomy but determined and unyielding."

On both sides of the Atlantic, the posters of World War II clearly had a different feeling than those of the earlier war. According to O. W. Riegel, World War II posters "were generally not as fervent, emotional or compelling." One reason was that people were disillusioned after World War I; particularly in view of the events just twenty years later, they wondered what the earlier war had accomplished. Furthermore, people were increasingly conscious of propaganda as something deceptive and evil. Riegel wrote that he thought the Second World War was "entered into with a kind of grim fatalism without heroics." He sensed a "diminution of exuberance and crusading zeal" of the posters from World War I.

Nevertheless, heroics were performed on the combat fronts and, in minor ways, by volunteers and workers at home. Poster makers produced both good and bad posters during World War II, with results that ranged from inspiring to silly and from vivid to pedantic. Critics can quibble about quality, but if those posters helped win the war—and there are good reasons to think that they did—they can't quibble about the results.

Chapter 8

America's Visual Landscape

Posters and Billboards Were Everywhere

Hundreds of millions of posters cascaded off printing presses across America during World War II. Who produced them? Where did they all go? And how did they get there?

The second question is easy to answer: The posters went everywhere, in homes, shops, factories, banks and post offices. Our modern concept of a poster is of a colorful print about 24 inches by 36 inches, but during the war, posters came in a variety of sizes, from small "car cards" (a mini-poster mounted in subways and trolleys) to huge billboards beside the highways. You would have to have been a very unobservant person in the deep boondocks not to have seen dozens of posters a day.

The federal government was a poster-producing dynamo, issuing posters in average press runs of 75,000 to 170,000. A quick survey turns up a few posters by the Department of Agriculture (one said, "Our carelessness—their secret weapon") and dozens by the Army, particularly its Recruiting and Publicity Bureau (RPB) and its Ordnance Department, which was extremely prolific. The Civil Service Commission issued posters to recruit workers (it needed millions of them). The Coast Guard's Graphic Unit produced several well-known posters. The Department of Commerce issued a poster that notified farmers about a crop census. The US Employment Service, Federal Security Agency, US Public Health Service, Interdepartmental War Savings Bond Committee and Merchant Marine all produced posters for their various causes and requirements. The Navy's Industrial Incentive Division issued safety post-

Previous page

Not quite billboard size but still huge, this patriotic poster hung from the ceiling of Union Station in Washington, DC, suitably backed by warlike figures from an even earlier era. As travelers marched to their trains, they could look up and see modern soldiers marching to battle. Gordon Parks made this photo for the Office of War Information in March 1943. Library of Congress.

The original caption for this photo is "Lonely soldier and recruiting poster on New Year's eve." Arthur Siegel made this photo for the Office of War Information in January 1942. Library of Congress.

85 MILLION AMERICANS *HOLD* WAR BONDS

Previous page
The Statue of Liberty was a ubiquitous symbol on American war posters, readily summoning up images of freedom. The statue itself was darkened after Pearl Harbor, and it wasn't relit until sunset on June 6, 1944. The emphasis in this caption may have been on the word hold, *since once folks bought bonds, the Treasury Department wanted to talk them out of cashing them in. Melbourne Brindle signed his artist's release for this poster on April 4, 1945.*

ers. The Bureau of Naval Personnel was the source of recruiting posters. The Office of Defense Transportation worked to discourage unnecessary trips with posters bearing captions such as "Could this be you? Don't travel unless your trip helps win the war."

The Office of Economic Stabilization pumped out posters explaining price controls and encouraging shoppers to support them. The Office for Emergency Management's Division of Information issued civil defense posters, as well as other varieties of posters; one proclaimed, "America's answer: production." The Office of Price Administration issued demanding motivational posters such as one that said, "Another tanker torpedoed off the Atlantic Coast. Should brave men die so you can drive?" Other conservation-related posters came from the Solid Fuels Administration.

All the military services issued posters, and branches of the War Department itself chipped in a few. Its Housing Center, for example, produced a poster that said, "Calling all rooms! 1,000 new War Department employees are coming and will need rooms! Have you a room to rent or share? Know of one that will be vacant? Call 2973." The War Department Safety Council issued several posters.

Posters came from the War Food Administration, the War Manpower Commission and the big daddy of all the "War" agencies, the War Production Board, which issued hundreds of iterations on the themes of work hard, work fast, and work smart. A 1942 WPB safety poster said, "Take care! Idle hands work for Hitler." A 1943 WPB poster said, "Big things from little ideas grow. Thomas Alva Edison, America's greatest inventor, worked small ideas into big ones. Speed victory, let's have your ideas." The WPB's Salvage Division also produced posters.

Sharp-eyed fans will find a few posters from the Office of Facts and Figures, predecessor of the Office of War Information. The OWI itself was without a doubt the premier producer of posters during the war, loosely following a pattern set during World War I. Back then, illustrator Charles Dana Gibson had been chairman of the Division of Pictorial Publicity, which was in turn part of the Committee on Public Information. Gibson's division produced more than 1,400 posters and cards for the government. During World War II, the OWI had its Artists for Victory organization of twenty-four artists' associations around the United States, with a combined membership of more than 8,000 artists.

The OWI had no peer in terms of variety, but if it did have one in terms of quantity, it would have been the Treasury Department's War Finance Division, which issued war bond posters. Most collections will contain more war bond posters than any other category of posters. Treasury Secretary Henry Morgenthau, Jr., was tremendously successful at enlisting America's artists for his war loan campaigns.

Government spokespeople and apologists went to great lengths to explain the necessity and importance of buying bonds. In the 1942 book *America Organizes to Win the War,* an essay by David Coyle was titled "How Can We Pay for the War?" It said, "If the war lasts long enough, say till the end of 1943, our Government may be spending about 60 billion dollars a year, out of a total national income of about 120 billion dollars." Before the war, Coyle explained, about twenty-five percent of the population worked for local, state and federal governments, so about that percentage of income took the form of taxes. During the war, however, "about half of us will be working for the Federal Government and getting our money from the Federal Treasury, so on the average we are all going to pay about half our money to the Federal Government."

That payment took both voluntary and involuntary forms, with bond sales falling into the former category. As historian D'Ann Campbell pointed out, "The gross national product expanded enormously during the war, but all of the expansion had to be channeled into military spending. The only way to do this without radically transforming the nation's economy was to first distribute the extra income to households, and then to take back about a third of that income through compulsory taxes, voluntary bond sales, and inflation."

Next page
On February 22, 1942, General Douglas MacArthur was ordered away from Bataan and smuggled out at night under the noses of the Japanese. Command was left to General Jonathan Wainwright. On April 8, American forces abandoned Bataan for Corregidor, which they surrendered on May 6. The American and Filipino troops captured were marched 65 miles through the jungle to a railway junction, where they were further sent to internment camps. Thousands died or were executed on the way, contributing another infamous chapter to the war's atrocities. Painter and WPA artist A. Brook did this spooky poster in 1943. The figure in the poster seems inscrutable, almost like a statue. The monochromatic coloring sets this poster well apart from the usual, vividly colored war posters.

Page 145
An artist named Wilkinsons did this war bond poster in 1942. The familiar minuteman logo, lower right, bears an unusual slogan: "The more bonds you buy, the more planes will fly." When a modern Navy pilot wrecks an airplane, he says he has sent it back to the taxpayers, an image that seems to directly descend from this poster's slogan.

144

Again, the pattern had been set—to a much smaller degree—during the First World War, when the five Liberty Loans (that war's version of what were called war loans during World War II) raised more than $32 billion. Artist James Montgomery Flagg, already a celebrity for his war posters, painted one poster on the steps of the Forty-second Street New York Public Library as a fund-raising technique for those loans.

During World War II, bond sales were consistently successful and more ambitious. In May 1942, sales exceeded that month's goal of $600 million. The target for June was $800 million and for July an even $1 billion.

Copy Policy for the 7th War Loan

In this internal memorandum from the Office of War Information archives, we see the strategy behind the scenes as planners grapple with questions they anticipate from the public. From this welter of concerns—the size of the loan, the status of the war, and the extraordinary demands on the audience—emerged simple, high-impact ads and posters.

There seem to be two salient facts about the 7th War Loan.

1. Its size will make it a jolt to the average bond buyer. The individual quota is 7 billion and the E bond quota alone is 4 billion—a billion more, in each case, than has ever been sought before. To illustrate what this means to the average bond buyer, consider this: a man earning $250 a month will be asked to put $187.50—cash—into *extra* War Bonds during the 7th War Loan.
2. Nobody knows where the war will be when the Drive is on. It's possible that, just as the Treasury asks people to lend more money than ever before, Germany will have fallen and we will be fighting Japan alone. In that case, the average fellow, not unreasonably, may wonder why he is being asked for a bigger amount of money to fight a presumably smaller war.

Obviously, from the point of view of quota-making, the 7th War Loan is going to be by far the toughest loan to date.

Now the Treasury did not deliberately set out to make its task difficult. There are good reasons why so big a quota was necessary at this time. Here are some of those reasons:

1. No matter what happens to Germany—or when—the cost of the war in 1945 will not be less than in 1944. Long-range plans and commitments—the fact that it is cheaper and quicker to give the Pacific forces new equipment rather than depend on repairing and shipping equipment from Europe—the cost of moving millions of men from one theater to another—the obviously greater problem of logistics—the increasing needs for care and rehabilitation of casualties—these, and a score of other facts mean that war needs will require about the same amount of money this year as last.

2. The danger of inflation is today not less, but more, acute.
3. There will be time this year for only 2 War Loans—instead of 3, as in 1944.

To sum up briefly, then, the situation is this:

We need as much money as we did last year.

And we are asking the individual to lend about the same amount of money as he did last year.
But we are going to have only 2 loans this year. And he must therefore lend in 2 chunks as much as he lent last year in 3.
In each of the 2 loans, therefore, he must lend more than he has ever lent in any one loan before.
It seems to us that the advertising's job in the 7th War Loan is to make that story clear to the average bond buyer.
The advertising should, of course, try to do more. It should try to put patriotic and emotional pressure on the reader to do his duty—as well as seeing that his duty and the reasons he is asked to do it are made clear.
There are undoubtedly many good ways to do this. One obvious way, for instance, might be to rely on interesting, timely, forceful pictures and headlines and leads for the emotional appeals—and then to follow this up with informative, "reason-why" copy. Although no one ad can do everything, it is desirable that, whenever possible, the advertising should also present the selfish reasons for buying bonds.

To sum up once more, the ideal ad would shape up something like this:

1. It would let the reader know at a glance that the 7th War Loan is on.
2. It would make clear to him what he is expected to buy in the 7th.
3. It would tell him why his quota is bigger than ever before.
4. Through a dramatic presentation of the inequality of sacrifice between the home front and the fighting front—or through an appeal to his desire to get the war over and get a son or husband home again—or through *any* strong emotional appeal—it would try to persuade the reader to buy his quota of extra bonds.
5. It would, when possible, give the reader the selfish reasons for buying extra bonds.
6. It would urge action through some sort of selling line or slogan.

147

Previous page
This poster, identified as WFD 72C, depicts all denominations of bonds, from $25 to $200. On May 1, 1941, the first defense savings bonds went on sale. After Pearl Harbor, the sale of bonds tripled, to more than $1 billion per month. Folks could also buy defense stamps, which varied in price from a dime to $50. All seven war loans met their goals, but most of the money came from banks, corporations and insurance companies.

In each case, the goal was met. By the time the Fifth War Loan was launched on D-day, June 6, 1944, the ante had been raised to $16 billion in bonds.

Another major source of appeals to the public by means of posters and other media was the National War Fund (NWF), an assemblage of humanitarian causes that were familiar to wartime citizens even before America entered the war. The story of the NWF is told in *Design for Giving*, a 1947 book by Harold Seymour. In that book's foreword, Winthrop Aldrich, president of the fund, wrote, "By the middle of 1942, we were fairly falling over each other in a complex and undirected effort to organize, to publicize, to solicit, and to give. . . . Seldom had so much good will been entangled in such a mess." For every country torn by war, ten groups were trying to organize aid for the POWs and refugees, and the American public was besieged with appeals from all of them; 596 different groups involved in foreign relief had registered with the State Department since 1939.

The cacophony grew to such proportions that in July 1942, FDR appointed a War Relief Control Board to sort out the causes and their relative importance. "By the middle of 1942 the situation was just about as well in

Next page
Two familiar slogans adorn this agrarian poster: "Back the Attack" appeared on dozens of versions, as did either "Buy More Bonds" or "Buy Extra Bonds." The logo of the Fifth War Loan features the minuteman silhouette, another familiar device used by the Treasury Department. Hoes and overalls—poster shorthand for farming—complete the symbolic scene. This poster was WFD 921, issued in 1945.

This small-sized poster features the ubiquitous combination of worker and soldier, although it isn't aimed at boosting industrial production, which might be expected.

151

Page 150
Georges Schreiber created this poster in 1944 for the Fifth War Loan. Schreiber was born in Belgium, trained as an artist in Berlin, and was noted for his ship and submarine posters for the Navy.

Previous page
Lawrence Beale Smith created this poster in 1942. Smith was born in Washington, DC, and worked as a painter, wood engraver and teacher. Along with the "Remember me?" poster, this was one of a well-known series produced by the Abbott pharmaceutical company, which in turn began as a series of fine art advertisements. Abbott had originally purchased seven paintings done by Thomas Hart Benton—which Benton called "The Year of Peril"—immediately after Pearl Harbor for a series of war bond posters. Abbott expanded the program to include a stable of nationally known artists and produced hundreds of oils, drawings and watercolors of American soldiers, sailors and marines in action. "Don't Let That Shadow Touch Them" was the first of the series; it draws effect in part from the worried, distracted expressions on the faces of the children. The limp doll in the girl's hands adds an ominous overtone, as well. More than 50 million copies of the Abbott posters were distributed by the Treasury Department, used in bond drives as well as in civilian defense, recruiting and production campaigns. As a result, the Army Surgeon General cited the Abbott series as "an eloquent contribution to the war effort that will be far reaching and everlasting," according to The Abbott Almanac.

hand as a greased pig at a midnight picnic," Aldrich wrote. The NWF's goals were to determine the nature and extent of war-related needs, to maximize the appeal for contributions and to channel the funds to the member agencies who needed them most. The basic question, Aldrich wrote, was, "Will this [project] help win the war or help win lasting peace?"

The National War Fund's publicity program included radio programs, advertising, magazine articles, posters, window cards and displays, car cards, motion pictures, newspaper articles, cartoons and photographs, speeches and stickers for restaurant menus. "Seldom has so much been seen and heard by so many people, so many times, at so little cost," Aldrich concluded. The fund figured it received about $30 million worth of advertising for about $1 million. Its fund raising appeals were successful, collecting $121 million in 1943, $113 million in 1944 and $87 million in 1945.

The NWF doled out the money it collected to thirty agencies, including war relief agencies from sixteen countries: Belgium, England, China, Czechoslovakia, Denmark, France, Greece, Holland, Italy, Lithuania, Luxembourg, Norway, the Philippines, Poland, Russia and Yugoslavia.

The USO was also part of the fund, getting a budget of $181 million. It was a federation of six agencies—the YMCA, YWCA, National Catholic Community Service, National Jewish Welfare Board, Salvation Army and National Travelers Aid Association—plus the affiliated USO-Camp Shows, which provided entertainment around the world. At its peak, the USO had 3,035 clubs and an average daily attendance of 1 million at USO clubs and camp shows. USO-Camp Shows played to as many as 700 groups per day, with 6,000 troupers, 400,000 performances and a combined audience of 202 million. The USO itself enlisted 1.5 million volunteers during the war.

The NWF eventually raised more than $100 million per year and represented more than 43,000 communities. It got help from a variety of sources. For example, the War Activities Committee of the Motion Picture Industry collected $1.5 million in theaters during a single week in January 1943. The New York State racing associations kicked in $1.6 million, and major-league baseball contributed $700,000.

As with so many other appeals that were answered by the American public during the war, the NWF's gave the average citizen a chance to participate and to contribute. Instead of backing the attack, however, the NWF helped in a humanitarian way. Harold Seymour wrote, "Perhaps it was your money that decorated the Christmas tree in some USO clubhouse in Alaska, that provided convalescent care for some torpedoed American seaman, that brought books or games to your own son in a Nazi prison camp, or sent an American ambulance driver up a Burmese jungle road. Or perhaps it was your money that put shoes on the bare feet of a Norwegian farmer, or saved some Greek child from starvation in the days before Athens was freed."

In addition to the government, numerous companies, civilian organizations and business groups issued posters, usually in support of similar national themes. Sometimes these posters were produced in cooperation with the government, and sometimes they were strictly private. For example, one 1944 poster by G. W. French said, "Uncle Sam sets the best table. Chip in for the chow. Buy War Bonds now." This poster announced it was "contributed to the Quartermaster Corps by the makers of Alka-Seltzer."

The Association of American Railroads jointly produced a poster with the Office of Defense Transportation that said, "War traffic must come first. Don't waste transportation."

The annual reports of the Association of American Railroads offer insight into the vast size of the various campaigns and the immense quantities of posters

Next page
The most successful war posters capitalize on combinations of striking images and clever captions. This poster has neither, and hence is among the less memorable war bond posters. Probably in an effort to appear conversational and informal, poster makers during the war developed a curious aversion to writing out the word them, *which as a result always appeared as* 'em. *Naval Historical Center.*

THE U. S. NAVY TORPEDO BOMBERS "DEVASTATORS"

AMERICA'S ★ ★
FIGHTING FORCES
Will Keep 'Em Flying
YOU Take Part
Buy
U. S. DEFENSE BONDS ★ STAMPS
Now!

153

The war was a wonderful time for slogans, and "Back the attack!" was among the most successful. This 1943 poster was by Georges Schreiber. Schreiber was born in Brussels, Belgium; studied art in London, Paris and Berlin; and was working as an instructor in New York when he created this poster for the Third War Loan.

This artist's preliminary sketch for "You Can't Afford to Miss" dramatizes how much more effective posters were when they added color and size. National Archives.

involved. The group issued 485,000 copies of six posters in 1940, 392,000 copies of five posters in 1941, 391,000 copies of five posters and 127,000 copies of three "special" posters in 1942, 324,000 copies of five posters in 1943 and 687,000 copies of five posters in 1944. Furthermore, the 1943 annual report said that the Public Relations Department "functioned in cooperation with the Office of War Information in the railroad distribution of the Government posters on a wide variety of subjects."

Another measure of the huge numbers of posters that were routinely produced during the war appears in a letter from Walter Conway, assistant chief of the OWI's Division of Production and Distribution, written to Hugh Harley of the Brewing Industry Foundation in New York:

Thanks for your letter dated January 25. We would appreciate it if you would pick up the 25,000 copies of the war bond poster cards, size 22″ x 28″, entitled "Attack, Attack, Attack",

which are now stored at the Efficient Direct Mail Service, 52 East 19th Street, New York City, New York. We have no direct contract with Efficient and we do not feel as though we should call upon them to make this local truck delivery in New York. Efficient has already been notified, however, to ship 5,000 copies to Mr. Atwill at Buffalo and they have also been informed that you will have a trucker pick up the 25,000 copies which are going to the Ruppert Brewery on Third Avenue.

We still have available 45,000 copies of the "Attack, Attack, Attack" cards and if there are any more which you can use, please let me know and we will make them available.

Next page
Martha Sawyers created this poster in 1944; it is identified as WFD 942. Sawyers was a writer and illustrator from New York and a member of the Society of Illustrators. She signed the artist's release for this poster on October 13, 1944. The model for this poster was a Guadalcanal veteran.

154

Previous page
This poster was created by Bernard Perlin of Richmond, Virginia, and was issued by the Treasury Department in 1943. Perlin started the war with the OWI's Graphics Division, went to occupied Greece in 1944 with British and Greek commandos as an artist-correspondent for Life *magazine, and ended the war in the Pacific in 1945.*

Civilian companies also designed and printed posters aimed at their own workers, usually as part of public-service campaigns, or to promote such topics as safety at work and high-quality production. A typical example was the Joint War Production Drive Committee of Hamilton Standard Propellors, which was a division of United Aircraft Corporation. The committee produced posters based on the winning entries in company contests.

The posters were mounted by store owners, plant supervisors, government workers and, to a great degree, volunteers. A typical volunteer was C. S. Johnson,

president of a company called Street Poster Service of San Diego. In August 1943, he wrote to the OWI, offering his services in the campaign to spread the word: "We have the advertising concession on the trash cans, in San Diego, Calif., which takes a half sheet poster, trimmed to 20x27," he wrote. "If your office would

This poster filled the cover of the first issue of the Oldsmobile Cannoneer, *a publication for employees, in January 1942. The publication had been called* Oldsmobile News *until Pearl Harbor, when the company adapted the name of its newest product as a more suitable title. The caption read, in part, "The history of warfare from time immemorial has been a history of extension of fire power. In the brief span of American history we have seen fire power characterized by muzzle-loading muskets and crude cannon of the Revolutionary days [advancing to the] faster firing and more accurate cannon [of today], more destructive long range weapons than ever before. America's output of guns, shells and cartridges was at a minimum only a few months ago. Today, thanks to the efforts of loyal Americans, like Oldsmobile workmen, this output is expanding at a pace well beyond that of days during World War Number One. . . . The nation's program of ordnance manufacture, without doubt, finds its center of gravity close to mammoth plants of the automobile industry." The front page had two articles, headlined "Olds' Slogan Stresses New Determination" and "Production of War Materials Is Urgent Need," and a small photo titled "Killed in Action," showing a former employee who had joined the 119th Field Artillery and had been killed in the Philippines.*

This December 1944 poster from the Association of American Railroads belongs in the category of simple, "we're doing our part" productions. It was AAR poster number 3194. The slogan wasn't mere hyperbole. According to America Organizes to Win the War *(1942), "In the subcontracting system, faithful efficient railroad service is a prime requisite. The various subcontractors on a gun or bombsight must have steady communication with the prime contractor. . . . For example, there are ten parts of a certain tank gun being manufactured by thirty-seven different subcontractors located all the way from Philadelphia to Davenport, Iowa," and all for a prime contractor in New Jersey. Association of American Railroads.*

send us about three hundred (300) a month assorted [, w]e would be glad to put them up and [donate] the space to Uncle Sam when not in use.... I am enclosing a picture of one of our cans."

The Boy Scouts distributed more than a million posters per month for the OWI. Several thousand theaters helped sell war bonds by showing shorts and trailers and allowing booths to be set up in their lobbies. Private citizens, servicemen and servicewomen, and other volunteers did their part, as well.

The Office of War Information produced a booklet titled *The Poster Handbook,* which outlined how to display posters. "Posting of official government posters is one of the most valuable contributions which citizens can make to the war effort," the booklet said. "It can be done in spare time at no expense and the results are welcomed enthusiastically in the community. They are great stimulators to other war activities, as well as a

valuable means of keeping people accurately informed." The OWI urged the formation of local poster committees, which could distribute posters and supervise their placement in public buildings, stores, restaurants.

A partial list of the companies that ordered copies of two posters—featuring Nimitz and Eisenhower—for the Seventh War Loan is an excellent index to the variety of businesses that displayed posters; it is also a fine, nostalgic dose of Americana: Blue & White Drive Inn (Boise, Idaho), Christensen Machine Company (Salt Lake City, Utah), Clark County Central Labor Council (Vancouver, Washington), Crocker First National Bank (San Francisco, California), Golden Quality Ice Cream (Wilkes-Barre, Pennsylvania), Nehi Bottling Company (Fairmont, West Virginia), Peck's (Lewiston, Maine), Rentschler Floral Company (Madison, Wisconsin), Square Deal Miller (Detroit, Michigan), Toledo Com-

This photo is from a book about the history of Oldsmobile, now in preparation by the staff at the Oldsmobile History Center. That book will show several similar scenes from Oldsmobile plants. Other work place posters said "Fire-power will win! And Fire-power is our business!" and "Is Your Car an Axis Taxi?" The war seemed to add impetus to every phase of work: attendance, safety, morale, innovation. Oldsmobile History Center.

munity Advertising Fund (Toledo, Ohio) and United Credit Jewelers (Little Rock, Arkansas), as well as American Fish Company, Brewers of Fox De Luxe Beer, Millers Peanut Butter and Salad Dressing, Ortwein Coal Company, Taystee Bread & Grennan Cakes and Veribrite XXXX Mints. The largest order came from the New York Savings Bank, for 1,200 posters. The smallest came from Bill's Drug Store in Detroit, for twenty-five.

Billboards also carried war-related messages in the form of gigantic posters, which is what they were called during the war. For war bonds alone, according to one wartime summary issued by the Department of Commerce, the outdoor-advertising industry's donation of "more than 135,000 posters or bulletins involving space valued at approximately $2,225,000 and carrying the Treasury message to an audience of more than 51,500,000 people represents the patriotic gesture of these advertisers."

And remember—that was just for the Department of the Treasury, and just billboards. It was just a drop in the bucket of the total number of visual reminders, warnings, commands, suggestions, hints and threats that reached Americans during the war in the form of posters.

The war bond and war stamp salesperson peeks through a wall of posters in the bank lobby in San Augustine, Texas. Several sizes of poster are visible, including what we would today call bumper stickers. At top left, an Uncle Sam figure inducts a nurse. The pair of posters in the middle was part of a larger series that depicted members of the armed forces from all the Allied nations. John Vachon made this photo for the Office of War Information in April 1943. Library of Congress.

During World War II, people used the word poster *to mean what we now call billboards. Motorists cruising near Lynchburg, Virginia, in early 1943 were confronted with this gigantic Uncle Sam, at the wheel courtesy of American Oil Company. John Vachon made this photo for the Office of War Information in March 1943. Library of Congress.*

159

Outdoor advertising record of war effort

The war years were a time of great volunteer effort, as well as a time of great tabulations of volunteer effort. Government agencies and private groups alike totted up totals and issued barrages of statistics. This table reports the contributions of the members of the Outdoor Advertising Association of America, Inc., as of January 31, 1945. The six-page report, which is in the OWI archives, tabulated the topics, value and client agencies for thousands of billboards scattered across the country. The careful enumeration of "value" may have something to do with the fact that some advertising expenditures were tax deductible.

Outdoor advertising record of war effort
Summary report

	Year 1944		January 1945		Future	
	Units	**Value**	**Units**	**Value**	**Units**	**Value**
National advertisers	271,876	$ 4,144,597.22	181	$ 3,110.06		
National contributions	81,749	1,295,337.00	6,640	127,296.00	50,009	$1,000,935.00
Local sponsorship campaigns						
War Savings Bonds & Stamps	93,346	2,313,867.85	2,742	68,001.60	12,198	314,234.96
Office of Civilian Defense	152	3,371.54				
War Manpower Commission	4,466	120,458.24	36	970.20	182	4,788.20
Forest Fire Prevention	887	18,573.54	35	731.50	13	247.50
War Food Administration	4,649	106,876.77	29	665.55	89	1,733.15
National Housing Agency	305	7,352.50				
Navy Department—Waves	3,545	84,970.34				
Red Cross	1,093	27,325.00	132	3,300.00		
Office of War Information	256	6,400.00				
Women's Army Corps	2,564	64,100.00	329	8,125.00		
Anti-Inflation	124	3,090.00	105	2,625.00		
	111,387	2,756,385.78	3,408	84,418.85	12,482	321,003.81
Local advertisers and local contributions (*)	63,453	2,411,705.64	838	36,834.32		
Corner posters (@ $2.50)	213,300	533,250.00			30,368	75,920.00
TOTAL	741,765	$11,141,275.64	11,067	$251,659.23	92,859	$1,397,858.81
War production or related work (*)		$ 5,938,026.83		$612,112.43		$6,360.749.94
		$17,079,302.47		$863,771.66		$7,758,608.75

(*) Based on individual reports received from association members.

A Cat and Mouse Story

First published in 1982
André Deutsch Limited
105 Great Russell Street, London WC1

Second impression 1983

Phototypeset by Tradespools Limited, Frome, Somerset
Printed in Belgium by
Proost, Turnhout

British Library Cataloguing in Publication Data
Rosen, Michael
 A cat and mouse story.
 I. Title
 823'.914[J]   PZ7

 ISBN 0-233-97484-9

First printed in United States of America 1982
Library of Congress Number 82-72953

A Cat and Mouse Story

An Old Tale

Michael Rosen

Illustrated by
William Rushton

ANDRE DEUTSCH

Once there was a very fierce cat who was running out of luck catching mice. She hadn't caught any for ages.

So one day she announced: "I am giving up chasing mice. I will never kill another mouse. The war between the cat and the mice is over."

And to prove it she said: "I'll invite all of you, all the mice in this house to come out every night, walk in a long line past me and take a piece of cheese I'll have ready for you. And you mice will all see how I keep my word. Not one of you will be harmed – I'll not touch a hair of your head. Not one of you."

And the mice — who up till then had been terrified of this fierce cat — agreed.

So that night the cat set herself up with her back to the fire and a piece of cheese for every mouse in the house. And all the mice came out of a hole in the wall, one by one, and walked past the cat and back into the wall through another hole. And the cat smiled and purred at each of them and they, in turn, bowed and nodded to her . . .

... "Good evening, Mistress Cat, thank you ..." took a piece of cheese and went back into the wall through the other hole. ... "Good evening, Mistress Cat, thank you ..." took a piece of cheese and went on, and so it went on until nearly the whole house-full of mice — maybe fifty of them in all — had passed in front of her and taken a piece of cheese.

But – just as the fiftieth mouse walked past her, her right paw shot out – as quick as a flash – and she grabbed that fiftieth mouse off the end of the line, and, as the forty-ninth mouse disappeared down the mouse hole, she held it tight; and the moment that mouse too had gone, she gobbled up the fiftieth mouse. Just like that.

The next night it was just the same. The cat announced, loud enough for
all the mice to hear: "Tonight I shall do the same. The cheese will be
ready for you. You shall see I am as good as my word – I have changed
my ways – I do not chase mice."

So that night, out came forty-nine mice, single file out of the hole: "Good evening, Mistress Cat, thank you ..." took a piece of cheese and went back into the wall through the hole ... "Good evening, Mistress Cat, thank you ..." took a piece of cheese and went on back into the wall through the hole.

This went on and on until the forty-ninth mouse came out of the hole. Then, just like the night before, as the forty-ninth mouse walked past, the cat's paws shot out quick as a flash and she pounced on that forty-ninth mouse and took him out of the line, just as the forty-eighth mouse disappeared down the mouse hole.

She held it tight, and when she was sure the forty-eighth mouse had gone
– she gobbled up the forty-ninth mouse. Just like that.

And so it went on – night after night she was gobbling up the last mouse on the line.

Well, with over a fortnight gone, the numbers of mice were getting down to about thirty, when one of the mice said: "I think there are fewer of us about these days." And another mouse said: "Funny – I was thinking very much the same thing myself."

There was another mouse there and that mouse said: "Well, it can't be the cat because she doesn't chase mice anymore."

But another mouse was there and she said: "I'm not so sure; I've never heard of a cat that can give up chasing mice once and forever."

So the mice decided to hold a meeting. Under the floorboards. And when they had all gathered together from all the different parts of the house – it certainly did seem as if there were fewer of them. And quite a few of the mice said they thought the cat was getting the better of them somehow, but they didn't know how.

"Has anyone seen the cat chasing one of us?" said one mouse.
No. No one had.
"Has anyone seen the cat moving at any other time when we file past her?"
"Just dozing," said one.
"Just sitting," said another.

"Are we all fit? Are we all well?"
Yes. They all were.

"Has any one of us died or run away?"
No. None had.

"Well then," said this mouse, "somehow or another she's getting the better of us. She's getting at us when we come for the cheese she's giving us. We have to find out how."

So they sat down and they thought and thought and they thought.

At last one of them said: "I've got it. It's rather complicated – but listen. Everyone of us can see the mouse in front – but none of us can see the mouse behind. So tonight let each of us make sure there's one of us behind."

So that's how it was. That night, like all other nights before, the mice filed out of the hole in the wall. Just as before, as each mouse came up to the cat each mouse bowed and said: "Good evening, Mistress Cat . . ." took a piece of cheese and said: "Thank you . . ."

But tonight, unlike any of the other nights, each mouse called out: "Are you there, sister?" or: "Are you there, brother?" and gave a quick glance over the shoulder. And each mouse replied: "Yes, I'm here, brother," or, "I'm here, sister." No mouse ever lost sight of the mouse in front and no mouse ever lost sound of the mouse behind.

Each and every mouse did it, right up to the twenty-sixth, twenty-seventh, twenty-eighth and twenty-ninth; and as they all filed back into the wall they collected together and waited for them all to be there.

"There you are," one of the hopeful ones was saying: "You see, it isn't the cat who's to blame."

And there was the twenty-ninth mouse just about to come in through the hole. "Are you there, sister mouse?" he said, and he glanced over his shoulder and the thirtieth mouse – she was gone!

"Help! Help!" he shouted, and all the mice came running out of the hole and their other secret holes and rushed at Mistress Cat.

She jumped back in surprise at seeing this rush of mice at her. She dropped the thirtieth mouse in her tracks; they rushed on at her, each one of them ready to nibble or bite any bit of her they could reach.

The cat turned and ran. She leapt up on to a window and was never seen or heard of again.

And that was how the mice saved the life of one mouse to save all.